One Muddy Hand

Books by Earle Birney

David and Other Poems (1942)
Now Is Time (1945)
The Straight of Anian (1948)
Turvey (1949)
Trial of a City and Other Verse (1952)
Twentieth Century Canadian Poetry (1953) (editor)
Down the Long Table (1955)
Ice Cod Bell or Stone (1962)
Near False Creek Mouth (1964)
The Creative Writer (1966)
Selected Poems: 1940–1966 (1966)
Memory No Servant (1968)
pnomes jukollages & other stunzas (1969)
The Poems of Earle Birney (1969)
rag & bone shop (1971)
The Cow Jumped Over the Moon (1972)
The Bear on the Delhi Road (1973)
what's so big about GREEN? (1973)
The Collected Poems of Earle Birney (1975)
Alphabeings and Other Seasyours (1976)
The Rugging and the Moving Times (1976)
Ghost in the Wheels (1977)
Fall by Fury & Other Makings (1978)
Big Bird in the Bush (1979)
Spreading Time (1980)
Words on Waves (1985)
Essays on Chaucerian Irony (1985)
Copernican Fix (1985)
Last Makings (1991)

One Muddy Hand: Selected Poems

EARLE BIRNEY

Sam Solecki, editor

HARBOUR PUBLISHING
MADEIRA PARK, BC
2006

Harbour Publishing
PO Box 219
Madeira Park, BC V0N 2H0
www.harbourpublishing.com

Harbour Publishing acknowledges the financial support of the Government of Canada through the Canada Council for the Arts and the Book Publishing Industry Development Program (BPIDP), and of the Province of British Columbia through the British Columbia Arts Council and the Book Publishing Tax Credit.

Canada Council   Conseil des Arts
for the Arts   du Canada

BRITISH
COLUMBIA
ARTS COUNCIL
Supported by the Province of British Columbia

Printed and bound in Canada.

LIBRARY AND ARCHIVES CANADA CATALOGUING IN PUBLICATION

Birney, Earle, 1904–1995
    One muddy hand : selected poems / Earle Birney ; edited by Sam Solecki.

ISBN 1-55017-370-7

    I. Solecki, Sam, 1946–   II. Title.

PS8503.I72O64 2006   C811'.54   C2006-903349-8

Contents

Editor's Foreword

"At worst, one is in motion; and at best
Reaching no absolute, in which to rest,
One is always nearer by not keeping still."
        (Thom Gunn, "On the Move")

Earle Birney (1904–95) began writing poems when Robert Service, Stephen Leacock and Lucy Maud Montgomery were bestselling authors throughout the English-speaking world, and he published his final collection, *Last Makings*, in 1991, the year Rohinton Mistry's *Such a Long Journey* won the Governor General's Award for fiction. By then he had become part of the Canadian canon—"David" alone would have ensured that—and was seen as an important figure in what might be called the formation of a Canadian literature. Although he wasn't directly associated with the Preview or First Statement poets of the 1940s, there's no doubt that he has his place among the fathers and mothers of Canadian modernism: Layton, Avison, Dudek, Page, Souster.

As literary editor of *The Canadian Forum* in the late 1930s and editor of *Canadian Poetry Magazine* from 1946 to 1948 he helped make Canadian poetry "new" by being receptive, as he would be throughout his career, to new voices and styles. As he wrote Al Purdy, "In my regime [as editor of CPM], both you and the 'ultra-moderns' as you call them, have a chance, as I believe in giving any craftsman a chance if he is a good enough craftsman... Every poetic generation has had to fight against the people who wanted to keep things just the way they were in granddad's day—that's true of all art, and all life. I'd rather be on the side of the present, the creative, the changing—but I'd still give a place in CPM for the good writer in the old forms, so long as he is good in them and has something to say. And I demand as much, if not more, from the experimentalist" (5 November 1947).

Although the entry on Birney in the *Encyclopedia of Literature in Canada* describes him as "among the two or three most important [Canadian] poets of the middle decades of the twentieth century," it also suggests that he is perhaps the most difficult of our moderns to bring into focus once we pass beyond the poems of the 1930s and early 1940s and "David," one of our few undoubted classics. There is certainly a continuity of themes and concerns—satire, social change, humanity's ambiguous situation in the world, nature, and poetry itself—but we don't have the impression that Birney created a distinctive poetic style. I don't think we can say of him, as we can of Layton or Purdy or Page, that he created a voice that is unmistakably there from poem to poem throughout his career. Instead there is what Desmond Pacey called his "eclecticism," which shows a poet less concerned with building incrementally on his body of work than with moving in new directions by remaining open to influences, experiment and movements, and being willing to rewrite poems. The early poems like "Anglosaxon street" and "Mappemounde" often look back to Old English alliterative verse; the post-war poems show a gradual shift toward the more colloquial style and free-verse forms that will be the norm from then on except for the experimental concrete and sound poems that appear as early as the mid 1950s.

One of the results of this formal and stylistic variety—it mirrors his peripatetic restlessness and frequent travels—is that it makes it possible to divide Birney's career into three overlapping periods corresponding roughly with the 1940s, 1950s and 1960s, and 1970–87. Though this periodicity can be discerned in the poems that follow—they are arranged chronologically—it is clearer if one reads his several volumes in the order of publication to experience the poems unrevised. While the revised versions are often an improvement, they simultaneously obscure Birney's development. The range of styles, voices, forms and approaches is impressive as lyric and dramatic poems jostle with reflective and satirical ones in a polyphonic mix. The connecting threads are the poet's inquisitive personae; the belief in poetry as central to our lives; the openness to new experiences; the continuing fascination with the English language; and the secular humanist world view.

One reader has suggested that a figure in the poetic carpet can be found in Birney's use "of mythic patterns that give context and meaning to poetic moments where the history we make illuminates the nature of our being." For Gary Geddes, "Birney's energies were continually engaged in coming to terms with his need for a social identity and with his separateness as an artist. Despite his involvement in the war and the universities, he always was an outsider, beset by internal and external forces that kept him from feeling fulfilled. He resented society's indifference to the artist and fe[lt] intensely that the artist has a cure for society's ills." Read more autobiographically, the collected poems can be said to constitute the narrative of a complex, often troubled life that spanned the twentieth century and that was rich in representative experiences.

The greatest surprise in Birney's development, as Al Purdy noted in a letter to his old friend, is the sequence of love poems written during the 1970s and 1980s for his last companion Wailan Low: "The 'Six for Lan' are the best love poems I've ever seen of yours. As if some bars to being personal had dissolved in yourself, and I think you have had such bars. But these, now, are lovely and delicate, they care about what they say. I am struck by the differences between my own love poems and yours. I am wildly romantic, at least to myself; but you are delicate and tender, with an overflowing sort of love" (30 July 1976). If Birney's earlier poems had often been personal and subjective, they had never been as openly intimate as these. The relationship rejuvenated him as a man and as a poet. It also prevented him from lapsing after his retirement from university teaching into a resigned old age in which he might have whined, echoing Mallarmé, "The flesh is weary and I have read the books."

This refusal to "go gentle into that good night" may also help explain the intensity of the interest in experimentation that becomes particularly important in his sixties and seventies. In *The Creative Writer* (1966), the poet who had begun steeped in the canon, offers a defence of Marshall McLuhan and "experimentation today": "Living art, like anything else, stays alive only by changing. The young artist must constantly examine the forms and the aesthetic theories he has inherited; he must reject most of them, and he must search for new ones. Literature is all the more alive today because it is changing so rapidly. In fact it's adjusting to the possibility that the printed page is no longer the chief disseminator of ideas, and that authors must find ways to bend the new technological media to artistic purposes." This is an attitude that, like his involvement with creative writing students at the University of British Columbia, kept Birney in touch with what the younger generation was doing. Though he occasionally thought of "David" as the albatross that prevented the public from giving his later work the attention it deserved, there is no doubt that it forms the cornerstone of Birney's reputation. "David" alone contradicts his despondent comment in "Cartagena de Indias, 1962" that "I... am seldom read by my townsmen." By its side I would place the following poems: "Anglosaxon street," "The road to Nijmegen," "Mappemounde" (a Purdy favourite), "Canada: case history: 1945," "Bushed," "Ellesmereland I," "A walk in Kyoto," "The bear on the Delhi road," "El Greco: *Espolio*," "November walk near False Creek mouth," and "For Wailan." It's an impressive and much-anthologized list.

It's worth noting that poetry, though it constitutes Birney's main claim on posterity's attention, was not the only genre in which he wrote. He wasn't quite what Roland Barthes would have called a writing machine, but he was prolific and produced two novels, several plays, three books of criticism, a memoir, and thousands of long single-spaced letters to correspondents around the world. Unlike Layton's, or Purdy's, Birney's influence is more diffuse, less easily defined. With the exception of Purdy, I can't think of another important poet whose work shows his presence. On the other hand, there's little doubt that his editing on *The Canadian Forum* and *Canadian Poetry Magazine* helped shift the direction of Canadian poetry at mid-century. Similarly his creative writing courses shaped a generation of writers coming out of the University of British Columbia. And an interesting what-might-have-been: had *Turvey: A Military Picaresque* been published unexpurgated in 1949, it might have had as liberating an effect on the language of the Canadian novel as *Ulysses* and *Lady Chatterley's Lover* had on the English and American novel two decades earlier.

The poems in this volume are drawn from *The Collected Poems of Earle Birney* (1975), *Ghost in the Wheels: Selected Poems* (1977), *Fall by Fury & Other Makings* (1978), and *Last Makings* (1991), all published by McClelland & Stewart. They follow Birney's arrangement of them in these volumes which was, in most cases, chronological even when he had revised a poem. When a poem is followed by two dates, the first indicates the date of original composition, the second the date of revision. The poems for Wailan break with chronology since he gathered and published them as "Fytte the Hindmost" (or Part Two) of *Last Makings*. Since the sequence has no overall title, I have taken the liberty of turning its dedication, "For Wailan," into one. I have retained the poet's preface to *Ghost in the Wheels* because it was his last substantive piece of writing about poetry and is relevant not only to the poems in that volume but to those that followed. Readers may be interested in knowing that the majority of the poems in this volume are taken from *Ghost in the Wheels*, in which the selection was made by Birney; I chose the rest. I have dropped two visual poems that appeared in *Ghost*: "Loon about to laugh" and "CHAT bilingual." In addition to poems from *Fall by Fury* and *Last Makings*, I have also added seven others from before 1977: "North of Superior," "Slug in woods," "Anglosaxon street," "D-Day," "Francisco Tresguerras," "Captain Cook" and "In Purdy's Ameliasburg."

The poems have required very little editing. In "Pachucan miners" I changed "Eürydice" to "Eurydice" (the umlaut crept in between *Collected Poems* and *Ghost in the Wheels*). I'm not sure whether "besteggiare" in "Once upon a hill" is a mistake or a neologism. The word doesn't exist in Italian (neither does "ridotto," which it replaced). Having checked with my friend Anne Urbancic, who teaches Italian at the University of Toronto, I've decided that it's either a playful neologism or a combination—a portmanteau word—of "bestemmiare" (to curse or blaspheme) and "festeggiare" (a raucous, loud celebration filled with expletives) that also suggests besting someone or one-upmanship.

The prose selections are from *The Cow Jumped over the Moon* (1972) and *The Creative Writer* (1966). *One Muddy Hand*, the title of the volume, is taken from "For Wailan" and was at one stage the title of *Last Makings*.

Sam Solecki
Toronto

Biographical Note

Alfred Earle Birney was born in Calgary, Northwest Territories, on Friday, May 13, 1904. His father William George Birney had travelled west on horseback from Guelph, Ontario and his mother, born Martha Stout Robertson, was one of many children of a Shetland fisherman. She was brought out to British Columbia by an older brother.

Earle spent the first seven years of life, which he described as a "Wordsworthian childhood," on a bush ranch near Ponoka, Alberta. An only child, he was taught to read by his father and entertained himself with the few books in the farmhouse. At seven, he was taken to Shetland by his mother to meet his relatives. He fell gravely ill but survived and returned, not to the ranch, but to Banff, where there was a school. In the summer of 1911, the family camped on the banks of the Bow River while William built their house on Squirrel Street. As a boy in Banff, Earle came to know mountains and climbing.

William enlisted in the Great War and served in France as an ambulance driver and stretcher bearer until he was discharged with shell shock in March 1918. No longer physically able to continue his trade of painting and decorating, William moved the family to Erickson, BC where they operated a fruit farm until Earle finished school.

In 1922 the family moved to Vancouver and Earle enrolled at the University of British Columbia. His plan to become a geologist or chemical engineer was diverted by a more compelling interest in literature, fired by the legendary teacher Garnett Sedgewick, and he changed his course of study, graduating in 1926. In the summers, he worked on mosquito control gangs in the Waterton Lakes and survey parties in the mountains. He climbed regularly with his friends.

In 1926 he started his M.A. at the University of Toronto. His father died in Vancouver while he was away. In 1927 Earle enrolled in the Ph.D. program at the University of California at Berkeley. He left Berkeley five years later, his doctorate unfinished, and went to teach English at the University of Utah in Salt Lake City, returning to Canada in the summers. He met Ken Johnstone and his sister Sylvia, both active members of the Trotskyite movement, and became politically active himself. He was married briefly to Sylvia Johnstone; the marriage was annulled.

In 1935 Earle travelled as a deckhand on a freighter to England where he continued his University of Toronto doctoral studies at the University of London. He spent his days in the British Library and his evenings working for Trotsky's Fourth International. In 1936 he travelled to Norway with Ken Johnstone to meet with Trotsky at Honefoss. They were arrested en route in Berlin for not saluting the Nazi flag.

At the end of 1936, Earle returned to Toronto, bringing with him Esther Bull, a fellow Trotskyite. He completed his doctorate with a dissertation on irony in Chaucer and started teaching at the University of Toronto. He was also literary editor of *The Canadian Forum*. On March 6, 1940, Earle and Esther married and their only child, William Laurensen, was born in 1941.

David and Other Poems, Earle's first published volume, written in the hours remaining after teaching and reserve-army duties, was published in 1942 by Ryerson Press. It won the Governor General's medal.

In 1943 Earle went to Europe with the Canadian army. He served in England, Holland, and Belgium as a personnel selection officer and returned with the rank of major in 1945. *Now Is Time*, his second collection of poems, was published the same year, and it also won a Governor General's medal.

Still partly disabled by the effects of diphtheria contracted in Europe, Earle worked for a year in Montreal as a supervisor with the international service of the Canadian Broadcasting Corporation. In 1946 he accepted a post as professor of English literature at the University of British Columbia, a position he held until 1965. At the university, he started a writing workshop that later matured into the Department of Creative Writing.

From 1946 to 1948, Earle edited *Canadian Poetry Magazine*. In 1947 he became close friends with Malcolm Lowry, who was living in Dollarton, BC, and published his poems in *CPM*.

In 1948 Ryerson published *The Strait of Anian*, a sequence of poems that treated every major Canadian city and region. The following year, *Turvey*, a picaresque novel drawn from experiences in the war, was published by McClelland & Stewart. It won the Leacock Medal for Humour, sold successfully and came out in pirated editions.

In 1950, Earle's mother died. Two years later, Ryerson published *Trial of a City and Other Verse*. The title piece, a verse play, was performed on CBC Radio. In 1977 the stage version of the play was published by McClelland & Stewart under the title *The Damnation of Vancouver*.

Earle spent 1953 in France on a Canadian Government Overseas Fellowship writing a political novel, *Down the Long Table*, published in 1955 by McClelland & Stewart. That same year, he spent the summer in Mexico in San Miguel de Allende with the expatriate painter Leonard Brooks and his wife Reva, the photographer. At this time, Earle was temporarily separated from Esther.

In 1958 Don Harron produced a stage version of *Turvey* in Toronto and Earle made his first circumnavigation of the world on his way to London to take up a Nuffield Fellowship. His travels resulted in *Ice Cod Bell or Stone*, published in 1962 by McClelland & Stewart.

In 1964 *Near False Creek Mouth* was published and Earle went on a national reading tour with Irving Layton, Phyllis Gottlieb and Leonard Cohen, sponsored by McClelland & Stewart. The next year, Earle and Esther separated temporarily again. Earle also left the University of British Columbia and assumed the position of writer-in-residence at the University of Toronto. He remained there until 1967.

1966 marked the publication of *The Creative Writer*, based on Earle's CBC Massey Lectures. *Selected Poems*, with illustrations by Leonard Brooks, was published by McClelland & Stewart that same year. In 1967 Earle went to the University of Waterloo as writer-in-residence, and *Turvey* was adapted into a musical by Don Harron and Norman Campbell for the Charlottetown Festival. The next year, Earle held the Regents' Professorship at the University of California at Irvine, and in 1969 *pnomes jukollages & other stunzas* was published by bp nichol as part of his grOnk series. In 1970 Earle was made an officer of the Order of Canada.

In 1971 *rag & bone shop* was published by McClelland & Stewart. One year later, Earle made his second circumnavigation of the world during which he completed a three-month tour of forty-three readings and lectures in Africa and Asia. *The Cow Jumped over the Moon*, a textbook about the reading and writing of poetry, was published by Holt, Rinehart & Winston of Canada.

In 1973 McClelland & Stewart published *what's so big about GREEN?* and Chatto & Windus published *The Bear on the Delhi Road* in England. In March Earle met Wailan Low, his partner until his death. They moved to Toronto permanently that summer, but one year later, Earle persuaded Wailan to defer her law studies to travel around the world for a year. They started eastward on Earle's third circumnavigation, ending in San Miguel de Allende, Mexico, where Earle started work on a literary memoir later published as *Spreading Time*.

In 1975 *The Collected Poems of Earle Birney* was published by McClelland & Stewart. Shortly after returning from Mexico, Earle suffered a broken pelvis and nerve damage when he fell from a high branch of a tree he had been pruning. He spent the summer in traction. In the same year, the original unexpurgated version of *Turvey* was published at the suggestion of Jack McClelland.

In 1977 Earle and Esther were divorced and *Ghost in the Wheels: Selected Poems* was published. The following year, *Fall by Fury & Other Makings* was published. In 1979 *Big Bird in the Bush*, a selection of earlier short fiction, was published by Mosaic Press. In the summer of that year, Earle took Wailan to Shetland and to the Isle of Bressay, where his mother was born.

In 1980 the first volume of *Spreading Time: Remarks on Canadian Writing and Writers* was published by Véhicule Press. During 1981 and 1982 Earle was writer-in-residence at the University of Western Ontario. He commuted from his home in Toronto to the university in London. In 1985 *Essays on Chaucerian Irony* was published by the University of Toronto Press and *Copernican Fix* by ECW Press. *Words on Waves*, a collection of Earle's radio plays, was published by Quarry Press.

On March 19, 1987, Earle's heart lost its rhythm and stopped while he was at the University of Toronto Press discussing a new project.

He was revived but it was too late to avoid brain damage. After months in the hospital, he went home for a year, but from 1988 to his death, he was cared for at the Queen Elizabeth Hospital in Toronto.

In 1991 the publication by McClelland & Stewart of *Last Makings*, the manuscript of which was prepared before Earle fell ill, proved Earle's belief correct that it would be his last book.

Earle died on September 3, 1995. His ashes were scattered with those of his mother, Martha, in English Bay near False Creek mouth.

Wailan Low

Preface
From *Ghost in the Wheels: Selected Poems* (1977)

People who just want to enjoy what follows should skip this preface. It's for "students" and "teachers," though of little use to them either, since I'm talking only about origins, how a few of these things came about. Autobiographical gossip. And I should like to say at the start that I don't any longer like the words "poet," "poems," etc. They've developed pretentious connotations. I prefer "maker" and "makings." They mean the same but the texture's plainer, oatmeal, not manna.

A high school girl comes up after a reading. Did it really happen to you? Were you engaged to a girl with violet eyes? (Yes, but only when she wore a violet dress.)... Or an undergrad engineer wants to know how my Lake Opal can be both in the High Rockies and close to Vancouver. (It's my prototype lake.) Where's that? (In the Big Rock Candy Mountains.) The distrust in his eyes darkens to conviction: I am a geographical moron.... The Canadian approach to "poetry" is often more literal than literate. I wrote a book to disprove, among other legends, the belief that I did push my best friend off a cliff.* But there are students, and at best one "professor of Can. Lit.," who still doubt my word. After all, I once climbed mountains, and I told "David" in the first person, didn't I?

The colonial past, still with us, inclines us to think that real invention takes place only elsewhere. Apart from Alexander Graham Bell and Stephen Leacock, well, who *was* there? When the new novelists write about what they know, the reviewers still hunt for self-confession, as they did in my day. I was once a radical and later a soldier; the anti-heroes of my two novels have therefore to be me.

As for my makings—if I didn't actually try on everything for size in an Australian Museum of Man, why do I say I would? Readers for whom science is science fiction, and astronomy astrology, will find everything a documentary, and humour an irrelevancy. Verses, in particular, may be thought of as only fragments from a diary, prettied

---

* *The Cow Jumped over the Moon* (1972), a would-be textbook on the writing and reading of poetry. It was universally rejected by the Canadian educational system.

up, except for real Lyrics like in Rock. But I have no absolutes, and can "explain" my own stuff only by setting off in a relative way; like the chap in the Einsteinian limerick, who returned the previous night. I start a making out of a yen to set down a momentary insight, a temporary "truth" relating somehow to me. But what turns out is always different, either because the perception got blurred putting it down, or luckily got sharper, ranging beyond the "reality" that triggered it and rumbling into a sort of dance with words.

I am taking a snap of a Thailand canal from a bridge one afternoon when a tiny naked boy runs in front of my camera. A man, presumably the boy's father, solicitous of the tourist, scolds him. I fumble up a coin and a bit of chocolate for him, the father smiles, the little one leaps from tears with a spontaneous dance of delight. I have a flash of identification with him that cuts through the veils of language, cultures, age. Later, writing it down, I become aware of many ironic, even pathetic, overtones. Earlier that day I'd seen bodies being dumped on the steps of a dying-house—cholera epidemic—and I'd walked on, the untouchable tourist, to view the gold-leafed temple-tombs and return for a swim at my American hotel to the sound of a jazz band. The night before I'd spent partly in talk with smokers in an opium establishment, partly watching a chorus of Hong Kong girls strip on a Bangkok stage. So this making grew from a moppet's jig to embrace my fear of guilty indifference to the human condition. Perhaps. At this moment I see it this way.

"Meeting of strangers" is a documentary—almost. Yes, I did get off a ship in Port-of-Spain and foolishly begin walking alone at dusk through the apparently deserted dockside. Yes, I will swear it (but there are no witnesses), I was nearly knifed and robbed of a six-dollar jacket. But I was white, and so looked prosperous. Colour me rich, colour him poor. And a taxi happened along, like a scene in a bad movie, and my thug shouted something I couldn't hear as I rolled away. But the driver couldn't either. So the last line, without which this piece would be only a fragment of travel-diary, had to be invented. The poem requires that jeering send-off, whatever he "really" said. Life presented me with a serio-comic puzzle and left out the key piece. I had to make one fit, in the interests of a different truth. It had to be a *Selbst-Ironie*, a self-mockery, for I was the fool of this scene.

The case of "Twenty-third flight" was similar. Here you could say every line to the last was true. A beautiful girl greeter was waiting at the steps of the plane to garland and buss me when I arrived, an aging greenhorn, in the Honolulu airport. She was from a luxury hotel and I was her only passenger, a fraud, a one-night splurger, flush for the moment on Lord Nuffield's charity to scholars. So there was a ritual, a contemporary fantasy, we had to conduct together. To make the piece, no details needed invention—only a style had to be found, to bring it all down from the commercially solemn to the mock-heroic, where again I must rightly play the fool. What classical voice should I borrow? I remembered my Flight Number (23), invoked the voice of King David, or rather King James's Committee, and at once the details of "reality" selected and ordered themselves into what I hope to be comedy.

Some youthful readers have expressed surprise, however, and some middle-aged ones disapproved, when they realized the Me of that making was actually fifty-four, and the one in "Curaçao" fifty-eight. Of course. This is the point of it. I am my own clown. Read Yeats's "Tower." So often it's the would-be critic who can't stand reality. Inside every healthy ancient is a trapped youth still lusting.

Sometimes the energy to spark a piece lies hidden till the last moment. One spring day in 1964 a friend and I came for the first time to Epidaurus. As we climbed the steps of the world's oldest theatre, I was trying to imagine what it was like to be part of an audience there for, say, a Sophocles opening 2,500 years ago. It would have been a raw new theatre then, whose erecting no doubt destroyed the peace of the fashionable rest home by the hot springs. But that hotel had been in turn a vulgarizing, an intrusion on an Aesculapian temple. If I knew more Greek history, I thought, I would try to make something—especially as I found, looking again in my guidebook, that the temple too was an invasion of the holiness of a primitive well. And now I am one of the two Canadians creating our own sacrilege, with the assistance of an unavoidable Greek guide. He has placed himself in the exact stone centre of the repaired *orkestra* and is waiting till we reach the top row and listen. Then he will drop the small pin he holds.... He does, and we hear it, sharing with all the audiences back to Sophocles, the marvel of classical acoustics. But all this isn't demanding a making from me. Something else is nagging, more ominous, not at all nostalgic.

Just before the pin dropped I remembered that a half-hour ago the guide asked me in careful English if it were true, as his morning paper had headlined, that Communist China had just made and set off a hydrogen bomb. He now, down at the amphitheatre's eye, we on the rim, have ears cocked for another pin.

If any of this seems dogmatic, not put in a relative way, it's only my clumsiness. I suspect I've said nothing about "poetry" that's more than half right. About all I can be sure about is that there are over a hundred makings in this book, none I think great and none I hope bad. They are supposed to be in chronological order of the first draftings—but it's hard to remember. Anything missing here and not in the *Collected Poems* is either sunk without trace or floating about waiting for a boat.

Earle Birney

NORTH OF SUPERIOR

Not here the ballad or the human story
the Scylding boaster or the water-troll
not here the mind   only the soundless fugues
of stone and leaf and lake   where but the brutish
ranges   big with haze   confine the keyboard

Barbaric the clangour of boulders   the rhythm of trees
wild where they clutch the pools   and flying with flame
of their yellow sap are the stretching poplars of May
running arpeggios up to the plangent hills

The horseman icecap rowelled the only runes
and snow-wild wind these eochromes upon
the raddled rocks that wear the tarns like eyes
within their saurian skulls   O none alive
or dead has cast Excalibur into
these depths   or if some lost Algonquin wooed
a dream that came and vanished here   the breeze
today shakes blades of light without a meaning.

Unhaunted through the birches' blanching pillars
lopes the mute prospector   through the dead
and leprous-fingered birch that never led
to witches by an Ayrshire kirk nor wist
of Wirral and Green Knight's trysting

Close march the spruce   and 'fir that weepeth ever'
the wandering wood that holds no den of Error
Silently over the brush they lift their files
and spear forever together the empty sky
Not here the rooted home but only discords
the logger sounds   tarpaper shanty scored
with lath he deeds next year to squirrel and spider
and little wounds upon the rocks the miner
makes and leaves at last to mending snow
The wood returns into its soil   the caribou
are blurring hoofmarks in the scrub   grey wolf
and man make flickers on the long horizon

This world that is no world except to hunted
purblind moose and tonedeaf passing hunter
yet skirls unheard its vast inhuman pibroch
of green on swarthy bog   of ochre rock
and the wine that gleams through the spectral poplar's bark
Not here   with hymn and carol blessed   Titania's
night   nor will this neuter moon in anger
pale for vanished rites or broken bough
For nocturne   hypnosis of lynx and owl
No heart to harden or a god to lose
rain without father   unbegotten dews

See where the unexorcized dragon   Fire
has breathed unwieldy lances from the wilds
for wars already waged   and planted one
charred pine to fly a pennant still   a husk
of golden needles—yet no mute or glorious
Milton finds Azazel here   no Roland
comes to blow defiance by this serpent stream

No sounds of undistinguishable motion
stalk the guilty poet flying   only
silence where the banded logs lie down
to die and provender the luminous young
The swordless rock   the heavenless air   and land
that weeps unwept into an icy main
where but the waters wap and the waves wane

CPR trains 1926/1946

SLUG IN WOODS

For eyes he waves greentipped
taut horns of slime   They dipped
hours back   across a reef
a salmonberry leaf
then strained to grope past fin
of spruce   Now eyes suck in
as through the hemlock butts
of his day's ledge there cuts
a vixen chipmunk   Stilled

is he—green mucus chilled
or blotched and soapy stone
pinguid in moss   alone
Hours on   he will resume
his silver scrawl   illume
his palimpsest   emboss
his diver's line across
that waving green illim-
itable seafloor   Slim
young jay his sudden shark
The wrecks he skirts are dark
and fungussed firlogs   whom
spirea sprays emplume
encoral   Dew his shell
while mounting boles foretell
of isles in dappled air
fathoms above his care
Azygous muted life
himself his viscid wife
foodward he noses cold beneath his sea
So spends a summer's jasper century

Crescent Beach, BC 1928

ONCE HIGH UPON A HILL

Up was down   was up   enchanted   & still is
or else to look back so far is to escape all gravities

Undergrad inseparables 4 years before in Canada
long bony me   longer bonier Slim
trails joined again haphazard here
on what a camping ground!   the Pacific's only City
(LA? actors & football colleges)   San Francisco   SF
(men of the world now   we never called it Frisco)
Our tent a 20$ furnished shack complete with fleas
propped on a gusty ledge of hill   no no   *the* Hill
(nostalgia overcomes me)   *Telegraph*   in 1930
before rich ladies conquered it with phallic towers

Stone eyes of Giulio's goat   the weird joy
that first morning in our wobbly hideout
(revolving now some 15,000 light-mornings under/over)
to see them glaring down from the primeval rockcave
old Giulio from Sardinia had built into his cellar
Down was up & sidewise & every map Italian
I'd prised the one window open to smell Freedom
Bohemia   our secret Latin Quarter
but what filtered through the dockweed demonstration
occupying the sheeptrack we had for lane
was purest ramstink   It punched me stumbling
through all the 6-yard length of our new Home
to the back porch   a broomcloset on stilts
where Slim's long nose was sniffing too   grape mash
steaming straight up from someone's blissful lilybed

It's taken some forty years for me to know which smells
& frenzies last: the sound of laughter's with them
though only Slim knows if that's what he hears now
For me the happy waves surprise   fade in on any station
or else I'd give up tuning in at all

I have to think hard what my worries were
tremendous surely for us both at 25   bad as now
Slim freshly jilted & dropped from a newspaper back home
his novels   my poems   lost somewhere on that virgin moon
Slim selling pickles in SF   me Remedial English in UCal
(both mainly to non-buyers)   o yes I'd flunked the Phoo Dee
for thoughts about Eng. Lit. not in the lectures
In 2 months I'd be a jobless foreigner
Something had started the papers called Recession? Depression?
& me engaged to Susie   fellowslave & holdout for a wedding
Yes   & all that hasnt left me one good stink for savouring

It was Old Berkeley   true   the air still innocent
of crude oil oratory or tear gas   Beside uptight Philology
a clean brook ran through woods (long since murdered)
where the few rebels walked   & Susie met me with a lunch
Sweet potato & eucalyptus   sick smells of academia
its boardinghouse & its sweatshops & fake scholars
Escape was on the Hill   Hell the bloody themes
could be marked in SF & ferried back to Berkeley (they were)
Meantime Susie   violet-eyed & fabulous   would wait of course

Lucky devils   it seemed we had it all   updown & sideways
or would have   once we achieved Sicilian mistresses
mastered Italian   made pals with the real citizens
those blackhanded stevedores from Naples   & Giulio...
Somehow only the mothers handled English
Used it when they collected rent or laundry   Except Maria
of the Lilies   who decided we were friends not Feds
& sold us something even she called Dago Red
four bits a gallon   you bringa your owna crock
It was our only breakthru   Funeral & shrill as crows
each morning over their tubs between the backyard ledges
Maria's blackskirt sisters cawed a secret language
while they swabbed & slapped & tore & patched the shirts
of all us dirty atheist *inglesi* who imagined
they could seduce their clean Catholic daughters
God knows we tried

Rejected, fucked only academically   selfunbelieving writers
whose aging mothers back home needed cash & careers from us
wernt we downcast as well as uptight   bewitched & buggered?
Is that how you recall us   my old/young fellow-batch?
I doubt it   We cast our balances from different figures
but the column stands   elysian on the Hill
If not   no matter   since nothing does but when it's there
& beatitude alive's too fast for savouring   it's drunk like water
Yet I would stake what's left of mine
your seesaw joy still spins   whatever length of telescope you try

Italians no   but maybe we could pass for artists
poets at least   We changed at evening to scarves
& climbed the crazy staircase-streets to Merto's
the only allnight blindpig on Telegraph
to sip the one beer we could afford
ignored by Billies banged or bearded & never seeing Merto
(turned out she was in Folsom on a legging rap)
Weekday mornings of course the world beheld us
falling headlong to the Embarcadero trams
Slim in his suit   for pickles   haymow hair slicked down
me spectacled & sweatered for the Berkeley ferry
(the already greying Bay   the still blue sky)
dangling yet more bundles of Basic Undergrad
margins bloodstained with my aborted lyrics

Ah but every helterskelter weekday we ended
crabwise on our Roman hideout   where proud as prentice guides
we clung somehow to our only City's only Matterhorn
Pharisees who knew not those on SF's other hills
hills trapped with streets   that blundered slapbang
over the cones of resurrected Francis
squealing with rollercoaster autos & trailing rails
for cable cars stuffed with their compromising tourists
On Telegraph Hill we had no streets   what's more no telegraph
no English   no rich   no cobbles   no cement
Humanists we moved in a sweet haze of deprivation
across the windstink on our blustering seacliff
No wheels at all   not even bikes   only the feet of cavemen
falling down a ladder jungle

& overhanding up again by wood lianas
to fire & sleep in doubly-blind stone alleys
It was what we'd grown souls for
this union with the last Hopi on a cliff
a Wop Cliff at that   long floated out from Genoa
& grounded like a wobbly hinge beside the Golden Gate
Come to think of it we never missed the Bridges
the Gate's own Self was there the way Drake saw it
the Bay open   to the Philippines
& latenight ferries served as well for us
as for the suicides we never thought of joining
—no boast in that   except of luck
Maverick fleas   too wild & fond of others' blood
(like those forever in our spavined beds)
to bite ourselves   we were busy riding the backs
of all our wooden centipedes jackknifing us plumb down
to separate jails at morning's 8   & up again to Life
at sundown   whatever Life is   when capitalized
Something that whirls at least   however senseless
The moment transient as smoke   yet tall in dreams
as when a great tree or steeple catches fire

It wasn't that we did a thing worth memorandum
failed to build Twat's Tower   or found the City Lights
If all on that Hill were still alive today
not one could recollect us   well Merto maybe
Merto the Great who came back at last
a gullvoiced gaunt Elizabeth the First   Virgin Hill Queen
hip & trippy 30 years too soon
She fell for Slim & bid us to her welcome-home besteggiare
We'd made it   Billies of the Hill now & till death do us

A week more & our shack was empty
I had a job in Salt Lake   Susie to join me in the fall
Slim meanwhile moving to her boardinghouse in Berkeley
We'd had a mere 3 months   a something   but no Eden
I think we refused to notice that we'd left it
As if needing some last symbolic gesture of betrayal
we held our final blowout   SusieSlim&I at the snooty Mark
on the last bloodmoney from my UC galleymasters

Or did we?   am I maundering now   of other girls timespaces
It's possible   Imagination makes numerals or Venus
from the seafoam   art's not the only way to simplify the past
senility will do   or plain laziness
I tell it so far as memory's concerned
& memory's now the only one concerned
a destructive child   breaking up *tabulae* for toys
There's some things we forget to keep in mind
& others we are mindful to forget
In the end we never bear to face the truth that nothing's done
that matters   unless it opens to the butterfly
the caterpillar planned   & even that's a thing of one-day matter

The biggest stars they say lack density
but some of them spin brightest in the lens
I'd call that Hill a crazy set we wandered into
& mimed our way along the scenic edge
juggling apprehensions & misapprehensions
playing kids   fools   vintage Beats   false
citizens   real lovers
in a comical-historical-pastoral goatplay called Cloudcuckooland
while all the showplace shot toward Centaurus

At least we had no time to invent our parts
try hero roles we could be still regretting
No doubt that growing old is feeling grateful
for the disasters chosen   not even visible
as scars now   except perhaps to others
Cockaignes recalled help me keep going
skindivers rise to dive again
Somewhere in my brain pan   that Hill stands
& turns me on   we wind again our long legs with the hollyhocks
the funstairs the housestilts the geraniums   & hold on
thinking we help to keep the crooked chimneys up
Perhaps we did   until a broker's generation came to topple them
It could be we brought Arcadia just the extra weight
that stopped the whole ramshack kaboodle from collapsing
in a cloud of sawdust goatshit grapeskins

Or say St. Francis   on his last American cliff
suspended gravity & time   while mortal & imperilled
we leaned *sans souci* down to love our falling likeness
in that fresh blue upside sky   & then we fell

Or did we?   & which way up?
A somersault perhaps   for I'd almost forgotten
it was Slim who stayed   who married Susie
I should ask you both   how you recall it
Was it like that at all?   or cant you hear me
& this is all a letter to the dead?   you don't remember?
No matter   whatever was   our ferris wheel went round
with gusto   its motion made a tune   a living one
allegro   not death's   his rigadoon wont sound
till all that turning stops   & we are neither sideways
up nor blissful down   but free   for all   or nothing

San Francisco 1930/Galiano Island 1970

MAMMORIAL STUNZAS FOR
AIMEE SIMPLE McFARCIN*

                           up
                  end
Ah but I saw her asc

                  upping breeze
            end
in the ass
There was a cloud
                  fall of kew
                              pids
their glostening buttums twankling
in the gaggle-eyed and (deleted) air

We had snuk away from the Stemple
            a   o
the whoop   lo   yah mongrelation
pigging their dolour
bills to the Kleigbright wires
We wondered at dawn
                           into the coca-
cold desert
                  t
where bitchy   o   souls of cacteyes
                  r
prinked at us
Then soddenly she was   gone
with cupidities   vamoostered
with pink angelinoes   O
mamomma we never forgueoo you
never your bag bloo sheikelgetting Ayes
loused   lost   from allhallow
Hollowood O
Aimee
Aimee
Tekel
Upharsin

Berkeley, California 1931/Montreal 1945

*Aimee Semple Macpherson, b. Ingersoll, ON, 1890, d. Los Angeles, 1944.

PORT ALBERNI TO GRIMSBY BY LIMEY FREIGHTER, 1934

I. Last Night in Harbour: Captain Bullthorp

Still red from thundering at the second mate,
young meek and milky Mr. Foote,
because a deck plank gave beneath a seaman's weight
scattering bagged potatoes to the scuppers,
the Captain stuffs the momentary spoils of land
into his tough old belly: fresh eggs and liver,
watermelon, a touch of whisky from his private
cache, into a sugar-heavy tea. Freddy the steward
scuttles out; the Captain in His messroom always
dines alone, square in the middle of his table,
square beneath his bridge. His portholes now
are blocked high with lumber chained to the fore-deck,
a sprawling prisoner any storm might free.
The Captain chews his meat in silence
and the deepening night.

II. Alberni "Canal": Departure

These firs already breathed when old
Pedro Alberni, Captain and Don
sailed into Nootka Sound to hold
with a hundred troops in his galleon
this pounding coast from Englishmen—
and quickly luffed away again
leaving only his stranger's name
to serve his channel and his fame

No man-grubbed ditch is this lank
lance the ocean thrusts unbending
deep into the scaly flank
of George Vancouver's Island: rending
glaciers alone have trenched
this giant gorge, and nothing less
than tilting continents have drenched
and drowned its floor in quietness
a hundred fathoms down   Today

the inlet's fretted crests are lost
in white obliteration, frost
of hillcloud sliding down to lay
a numb annihilation straight
along the mountain's bony knees
Above that line the gauzy trees
dissolve like ghosts caught out too late

III.   ka pass age alaska passage ALASKA PASSAGE alaska passage alas

our ship seems reefed
and only the land comes swimming past alaska pass

the firs tramp through downwards the fog in green crescendo the foRE/

SHore'S pleD cOMmotion of

bristled
ROCKS

drift

and blanching

uP from a spew of splinters & BaRK A Logchute Arrows

(one mark of few that men have scribbled
on this lucky palimpsest of ranges)

at times a shake-built shack exchanges
passive stares with Come & Gone
or eyeless waits with stoven side
to
slide its bones in a
green tide

age alaska passage alaska passage alaska passage alas-ka pass

Alberni Canal 1934/1947/1960

DAVID

I

David and I that summer cut trails on the Survey.
All week in the valley for wages, in air that was steeped
In the wail of mosquitoes, but over the sunalive week-ends
We climbed, to get from the ruck of the camp, the surly

Poker, the wrangling, the snoring under the fetid
Tents, and because we had joy in our lengthening coltish
Muscles, and mountains for David were made to see over,
Stairs from the valleys and steps to the sun's retreats.

II

Our first was Mount Gleam. We hiked in the long afternoon
To a curling lake and lost the lure of the faceted
Cone in the swell of its sprawling shoulders. Past
The inlet we grilled our bacon, the strips festooned

On a poplar prong, in the hurrying slant of the sunset.
Then the two of us rolled in the blanket while round us the cold
Pines thrust at the stars. The dawn was a floating
Of mists till we reached to the slopes above timber, and won

To snow like fire in the sunlight. The peak was upthrust
Like a fist in a frozen ocean of rock that swirled
Into valleys the moon could be rolled in. Remotely unfurling
Eastward the alien prairie glittered. Down through the dusty

Skree on the west we descended, and David showed me
How to use the give of shale for giant incredible
Strides. I remember, before the larches' edge,
That I jumped a long green surf of juniper flowing

Away from the wind, and landed in gentian and saxifrage
Spilled on the moss. Then the darkening firs
And the sudden whirring of water that knifed down a fern-hidden
Cliff and splashed unseen into mist in the shadows.

III

One Sunday on Rampart's arête a rainsquall caught us,
And passed, and we clung by our blueing fingers and bootnails
An endless hour in the sun, not daring to move
Till the ice had steamed from the slate. And David taught me

How time on a knife-edge can pass with the guessing of fragments
Remembered from poets, the naming of strata beside one,
And matching of stories from schooldays.... We crawled astride
The peak to feast on the marching ranges flagged

By the fading shreds of the shattered stormcloud. Lingering
There it was David who spied to the south, remote,
And unmapped, a sunlit spire on Sawback, an overhang
Crooked like a talon. David named it the Finger.

That day we chanced on the skull and the splayed white ribs
Of a mountain goat underneath a cliff-face, caught
On a rock. Around were the silken feathers of hawks.
And that was the first I knew that a goat could slip.

IV

And then Inglismaldie. Now I remember only
The long ascent of the lonely valley, the live
Pine spirally scarred by lightning, the slicing pipe
Of invisible pika, and great prints, by the lowest

Snow, of a grizzly. There it was too that David
Taught me to read the scroll of coral in limestone
And the beetle-scal in the shale of ghostly trilobites,
Letters delivered to man from the Cambrian waves.

V

On Sundance we tried from the col and the going was hard.
The air howled from our feet to the smudged rocks
And the papery lake below. At an outthrust we baulked
Till David clung with his left to a dint in the scarp,

Lobbed the iceaxe over the rocky lip,
Slipped from his holds and hung by the quivering pick,
Twisted his long legs up into space and kicked
To the crest. Then grinning, he reached with his freckled wrist

And drew me up after. We set a new time for that climb.
That day returning we found a robin gyrating
In grass, wing-broken. I caught it to tame but David
Took and killed it, and said, "Could you teach it to fly?"

VI

In August, the second attempt, we ascended The Fortress,
By the forks of the Spray we caught five trout and fried them
Over a balsam fire. The woods were alive
With the vaulting of mule-deer and drenched with clouds all the
    morning,

Till we burst at noon to the flashing and floating round
Of the peaks. Coming down we picked in our hats the bright
And sunhot raspberries, eating them under a mighty
Spruce, while a marten moving like quicksilver scouted us.

VII

But always we talked of the Finger on Sawback, unknown
And hooked, till the first afternoon in September we slogged
Through the musky woods, past a swamp that quivered with frog-
    song,
And camped by a bottle-green lake. But under the cold

Breath of the glacier sleep would not come, the moonlight
Etching the Finger. We rose and trod past the feathery
Larch, while the stars went out, and the quiet heather
Flushed, and the skyline pulsed with the surging bloom

Of incredible dawn in the Rockies. David spotted
Bighorns across the moraine and sent them leaping
With yodels the ramparts redoubled and rolled to the peaks,
And the peaks to the sun. The ice in the morning thaw

Was a gurgling world of crystal and cold blue chasms,
And seracs that shone like frozen saltgreen waves.
At the base of the Finger we tried once and failed. Then David
Edged to the west and discovered the chimney; the last

Hundred feet we fought the rock and shouldered and kneed
Our way for an hour and made it. Unroping we formed
A cairn on the rotting tip. Then I turned to look north
At the glistening wedge of giant Assiniboine, heedless

Of handhold. And one foot gave. I swayed and shouted.
David turned sharp and reached out his arm and steadied me,
Turning again with a grin and his lips ready
To jest. But the strain crumbled his foothold. Without

A gasp he was gone. I froze to the sound of grating
Edge-nails and fingers, the slither of stones, the lone
Second of silence, the nightmare thud. Then only
The wind and the muted beat of unknowing cascades.

VIII

Somehow I worked down the fifty impossible feet
To the ledge, calling and getting no answer but echoes
Released in the cirque, and trying not to reflect
What an answer would mean. He lay still, with his lean

Young face upturned and strangely unmarred, but his legs
Splayed beneath him, beside the final drop,
Six hundred feet sheer to the ice. My throat stopped
When I reached him, for he was alive. He opened his grey

Straight eyes and brokenly murmured "over... over."
And I, feeling beneath him a cruel fang
Of the ledge thrust in his back, but not understanding,
Mumbled stupidly, "Best not to move," and spoke

Of his pain. But he said, "I can't move... If only I felt
Some pain." Then my shame stung the tears to my eyes
As I crouched, and I cursed myself, but he cried,
Louder, "No, Bobbie! Don't ever blame yourself.

I didn't test my foothold." He shut the lids
Of his eyes to the stare of the sky, while I moistened his lips
From our water flask and tearing my shirt into strips
I swabbed the shredded hands. But the blood slid

From his side and stained the stone and the thirsting lichens,
And yet I dared not lift him up from the gore
Of the rock. Then he whispered, "Bob, I want to go over!"
This time I knew what he meant and I grasped for a lie

And said, "I'll be back here by midnight with ropes
And men from the camp and we'll cradle you out." But I knew
That the day and the night must pass and the cold dews
Of another morning before such men unknowing

The ways of mountains could win to the chimney's top.
And then, how long? And he knew.... and the hell of hours
After that, if he lived till we came, roping him out.
But I curled beside him and whispered, "The bleeding will stop.

You can last." He said only, "Perhaps.... For what? A wheelchair,
Bob?" His eyes brightening with fever upbraided me.
I could not look at him more and said, "Then I'll stay
With you." But he did not speak, for the clouding fever.

I lay dazed and stared at the long valley,
The glistening hair of a creek on the rug stretched
By the firs, while the sun leaned round and flooded the ledge,
The moss, and David still as a broken doll.

I hunched to my knees to leave, but he called and his voice
Now was sharpened with fear. "For Christ's sake push me over!
If I could move.... Or die.... " The sweat ran from his forehead,
But only his eyes moved. A hawk was buoying

Blackly its wings over the wrinkled ice.
The purr of a waterfall rose and sank with the wind.
Above us climbed the last joint of the Finger
Beckoning bleakly the wide indifferent sky.

Even then in the sun it grew cold lying there.... And I knew
He had tested his holds. It was I who had not.... I looked
At the blood on the ledge, and the far valley. I looked
At last in his eyes. He breathed, "I'd do it for you, Bob."

38

IX

I will not remember how nor why I could twist
Up the wind-devilled peak, and down through the chimney's empty
Horror, and over the traverse alone. I remember
Only the pounding fear I would stumble on It

When I came to the grave-cold maw of the bergschrund... reeling
Over the sun-cankered snowbridge, shying the caves
In the névé... the fear, and the need to make sure It was there
On the ice, the running and falling and running, leaping

Of gaping greenthroated crevasses, alone and pursued
By the Finger's lengthening shadow. At last through the fanged
And blinding seracs I slid to the milky wrangling
Falls at the glacier's snout, through the rocks piled huge

On the humped moraine, and into the spectral larches,
Alone. By the glooming lake I sank and chilled
My mouth but I could not rest and stumbled still
To the valley, losing my way in the ragged marsh.

I was glad of the mire that covered the stains, on my ripped
Boots, of his blood, but panic was on me, the reek
Of the bog, the purple glimmer of toadstools obscene
In the twilight. I staggered clear to a firewaste, tripped

And fell with a shriek on my shoulder. It somehow eased
My heart to know I was hurt, but I did not faint
And I could not stop while over me hung the range
Of the Sawback. In blackness I searched for the trail by the creek

And found it.... My feet squelched a slug and horror
Rose again in my nostrils. I hurled myself
Down the path. In the woods behind some animal yelped.
Then I saw the glimmer of tents and babbled my story.

I said that he fell straight to the ice where they found him,
And none but the sun and incurious clouds have lingered
Around the marks of that day on the ledge of the Finger,
That day, the last of my youth, on the last of our mountains.

Toronto 1940

39

VANCOUVER LIGHTS

About me the night   moonless   wimples the mountains
wraps ocean   land   air   and mounting
sucks at the stars   The city   throbbing below
webs the sable peninsula   The golden
strands overleap the seajet   by bridge and buoy
vault the shears of the inlet   climb the woods
toward me   falter   and halt   Across to the firefly
haze of a ship on the gulf's erased horizon
roll the lambent spokes of a lighthouse

Through the feckless years we have come to the time
when to look on this quilt of lamps is a troubling delight
Welling from Europe's bog   through Africa flowing
and Asia   drowning the lonely lumes on the oceans
tiding up over Halifax   now to this winking
outpost comes flooding the primal ink

On this mountain's brutish forehead with terror of space
I stir   of the changeless night and the stark ranges
of nothing   pulsing down from the beyond and between
the fragile planets   We are a spark beleaguered
by darkness   this twinkle we make in a corner of emptiness
how shall we utter our fear that the black Experimentress
will never in the range of her microscope find it?   Our Phoebus
himself is a bubble that dries on Her slide   while the Nubian
wears for an evening's whim a necklace of nebulae

Yet we must speak   we the unique glowworms
Out of the waters and rocks of our little world
we conjured these flames   hooped these sparks
by our will   From blankness and cold we fashioned stars
to our size   and signalled Aldebaran
This must we say   whoever may be to hear us
if murk devour   and none weave again in gossamer:

                                    These rays were ours
we made and unmade them   Not the shudder of continents
doused us   the moon's passion   nor crash of comets
In the fathomless heat of our dwarfdom   our dream's combustion
we contrived the power the blast that snuffed us
No one bound Prometheus   Himself he chained
and consumed his own bright liver   O stranger
Plutonian   descendant   or beast in the stretching night—
there was light

1941

WAR WINTERS

Sun
proud Bessemer   peltwarmer beauty
these winters yoke us   We scan sky for you
The dun droppings blur   we drown in snow
Is this tarnished chimneyplug   in a tenantless room
this sucked wafer   white simpleton
you?

Not
chiefly the months   mould you heartcharmer
to scant hammerdent   on hardiron sky
not alone latitude   to lodgers on this
your slantwhirling lackey   lifecrusted satellite
this your own wrynecked   woedealing
world

Hazelton Avenue, Toronto 1941

ANGLOSAXON STREET

Dawndrizzle ended   dampness steams from
blotching brick and   blank plasterwaste
Faded housepatterns   hoary and finicky
unfold stuttering   stick like a phonograph

Here is a ghetto   gotten for goyim
O with care denuded   of nigger and kike
No coonsmell rankles   reeks only cellarrot
attar of carexhaust   catcorpse and cookinggrease
Imperial hearts   heave in this haven
Cracks across windows   are welded with slogans
There'll Always Be An England   enhances geraniums
and V's for Victory   vanquish the housefly

Ho! with climbing sun   march the bleached beldames
festooned with shopping bags   farded flatarched
bigthewed Saxonwives   stepping over buttrivers
waddling back wienerladen   to suckle smallfry

Hoy! with sunslope   shrieking over hydrants
flood from learninghall   the lean fingerlings
Nordic nobblecheeked   not all clean of nose
leaping Commandowise   into leprous lanes

What! after whistleblow!   spewed from wheelboat
after daylong doughtiness   dire handplay
in sewertrench or sandpit   come Saxonthegns
Junebrown Jutekings   jawslack for meat

Sit after supper   on smeared doorsteps
not humbly swearing   hatedeeds on Huns
profiteers politicians   pacifists Jews

Then by twobit magic   to muse in movie
unlock picturehoard   or lope to alehall
soaking bleakly   in beer skittleless

Home again to hotbox   and humid husbandhood
in slumbertrough adding   sleepily to Anglekin
Alongside in lanenooks   carling and leman
caterwaul and clip   careless of Saxonry
with moonglow and haste   and a higher heartbeat

Slumbers now slumtrack   unstinks cooling
waiting brief for milkmaid   mornstar and worldrise

Toronto 1942

THE ROAD TO NIJMEGEN*

December my dear on the road to Nijmegen
between the stones and the bitten sky
was your face

Not yours at first
but only the countenance of lank canals
and gathered stares
(too rapt to note my passing)
of graves with frosted billy-tins for epitaphs
bones of tanks beside the stoven bridges

and old men in the mist
hacking the last chips
from a boulevard of stumps

These for miles and the fangs of homes
where women wheeled in the wind
on the tireless rims of their cycles
like tattered sailboats,
tossing over the cobbles

and the children
groping in gravel for knobs of coal
or clustered like wintered flies
at the back of messhuts
their legs standing like dead stems out of their clogs

Numbed on the long road to mangled Nijmegen
I thought that only the living of others assures us
the gentle and true we remember as trees walking
Their arms reach down from the light of kindness
into this Lazarus tomb

So peering through sleet as we neared Nijmegen
I glimpsed the rainbow arch of your eyes
Over the clank of the jeep
your quick grave laughter
outrising at last the rockets
brought me what spells I repeat

as I travel this road
that arrives at no future
and what creed I can bring
to our daily crimes
to this guilt
in the griefs of the old
and the graves of the young

*Nijmegen was in 1944–5 the town at the tip of the Canadian salient in Holland, connected with rearward troops by a single much-bombed highway. The area had been the scene of tank battles, artillery duels, air raids, buzz-bomb and V-2 rocket attacks. It had also been denuded of trees, coal and foodstocks by the retreating Germans. The winter was in all Europe one of the coldest of the century.

THIS PAGE MY PIGEON
(for esther)

This page is my pigeon sailing
out of the blasted Now to you
my greenest past   my rivered future
See   round his leg snug   love's cylinder

come from this world of wild undoing
from all this quarrel of iron and growth
Weaving by snake-spit of ack-ack and robot's
roar-horror   up past the beautiful brutal

bombers floating like flakes of mica
leaps my faithful feathered one   soars
through the haired and dirty clouds of the war
cleaving cleanly the selfcentred sky

Under apathetic suns and over
the pointless ocean he arrows   off
to the one unlosable loft
What does he say for me   what brings my homer?

Says that your voice still waters my memory
your eyes are leads to the wide light
that will be   Swears you are part of the rightness
of hills   the saneness of music and hemlocks

Says the giraffish dockweed   loneliness
was lopped away long ago   burned in your vaulting fire
when first you gardened me   Now this gyring
windstorm of absence whirls ashes up only

Windseed is barren   takes no truehold
in heart tendrilled tight with existence of you

Portsmouth 1944

D-DAY

Between the pasturing clouds
the skies winked blue today
as yesterday
Above the glinting flints
along the hazel path
the buttercups were babied in the breeze
and lupins ladied
all the air with scent
as yesterday
I had to stray
a mile along the Pilgrim's Way
past hawthorn mothed
by roses 'unofficial'
and through lost Chaucer's
soft sweet grass
before a host of hopvines
green and writhing
before a poppy-wounded
regiment of rye
forced laggard heart
beyond the sunset pass
to beat with blasted beaches
in the D-Day tempo
to throb *maestoso*
with the mightiest oratorio
in all the long
wrong music
of man's mind

Hog's Back, Surrey 6 June 1944

45

YOUNG VETERANS

They return with new cells, old eyes
to their strange children and older wives
They try to be as they were remembered
or to contrive how they are rendered
and failing are themselves again....

Memory of deeds and of their causes
rusts with the capbadge in the closet
Hates like souvenirs are thumbed awhile
then lost in moving or by the playing child....

These soldiers merge and move with all of us
toward whatever mystery
bemused that fatal pliant fish
who first forgot the sea

Christie Military Hospital, Toronto 1945

MAPPEMOUNDE

No not this old   whalehall can whelm us
shiptamed gullgraced   soft to our glidings
Harrows that mere more   which squares our map
See in its north   where scribe has marked *mermen*
shore-sneakers who croon   to the seafarer's girl
next year's gleewords   East and west *nadders*
flamefanged bale-twisters   their breath dries up tears
chars in the breast-hoard   the brave picture-faces
Southward *Cetegrande* that   sly beast who sucks in
with whirlwind also   the wanderer's pledges
That sea is hight Time   it hems all hearts' landtrace
Men say the redeless   reaching its bounds
topple in maelstrom   tread back never
Adread in that mere   we drift to map's end

Hospital Ship El Nil, *Atlantic 1945*

46

ATLANTIC DOOR

Through or over the deathless feud
of the cobra sea and the mongoose wind
you must fare to reach us
through hiss and throttle come
where the great ships are scattered twigs
on a green commotion
where the plane is a fugitive mote
in the stare of the sun
Come by a limbo of motion humbled
under cliffs of cloud
and over gargantuan whalehalls
In this lymph's abyss a billion
years of spawning and dying have passed
and will pass without ministration of man
For all the red infusions of sailors
veins of vikings lost and matelots
haemoglobin of Gilbert's hearties and Jellicoe's
for all blood seeping from corvette and sealer
from sodden hulls of *Hood* and *Titanic*
still do these waves when the gale snaps them
fracture white as the narwhal's tusk
Come then trailing whatever pattern
of gain or solace and think no more than you must
of the simple unhuman truth of this emptiness
that down deep below the lowest pulsing
of primal cell
tar-dark and dead
lie the bleak and forever capacious tombs of the sea

Grand Banks 1945

TRANSCONTINENTAL

Crawling across this sometime garden
now in our trainbeds like clever nits
in a plush caterpillar should we take time
to glance from our dazzle of magazines
and behold this great green girl grown sick
with man   sick with the likes of us?

Toes mottled long ago by soak of seaports
ankles rashed with stubble
belly papulous with stumps?
And should we note where maggoting miners
still bore her bones to feed our crawling host
or consider the scars across her breasts
the scum of tugs upon her lakeblue eyes
the clogging logs within her blood—
in the doze between our magazines?

For certainly she is ill   her skin
is creased with our coming and going
and we trail in her face the dark breath of her dooming

She is too big and strong perhaps to die
of this disease but she grows quickly old
this lady   old with us—
nor have we any antibodies for her aid
except our own.

New Brunswick 1945

48

MAN ON A TRACTOR

What does he think
that man on a tractor
unrolling the earth's flesh
in multiple ribands behind him?
Sometimes perhaps he reckons
while rhythmic spirals of dust whirl to his throat
the hours and their fractions
till by the well he can hose his puckering skin
    By God it's going to be different now
    with a wife at the end of day
    and turning my own soil

His thoughts jog back through the burglared years
as he wheels at a corner and faces
across the coulee the barn of his old boss
remembers the long oilcloth at supper
busy with flies and chewing
the draggletailed farmwife doling old ham and custard
This is better for sure
though the brute sun
burns him still on the naked land
and the light will dim before the chores of the day are done

Yet the throb of the iron seat
blurs in his mind with the days when he bruised his bones
driving in lines more devious
clamouring over Italian cobbles or scrub or bodies
rocking as he coughed in the fumes and waited
a shell's conclusion
Peering through olives he sometimes had fancied a flash
of chequered Albertan stubble or dreamt from a ruin
the gasoline hatbox marking the lay of this town
where the giant nostril of war inhaled and exhaled him
    Now with the prairie breeze around me
    why do I daydream of tanks
    and gulping compo with buddies
    scattered forever or dead?

He loved that clanking demon no more than the shark
is loved by its pilot-fish
What does he want?
Does he need for ever to hunt and be hunted?
    I have come through with my hands and feet
    and won the right to plow black earth of my own
yet sprouting thicker than wheat, he thinks,
are the towers of its traders

And now the shake of the tractor blurs to the flatcar
he and his brother rode through the stammering prairie
into the fountaining woods and the mountains
They had watched the olive lakes unreel
and the flying rivers milked
with the grist of the glaciers
inching down from the dazzling peaks
    Could it be only eight years ago
    that we munched a stale handout
    planned against yardbulls ahead
    and shivering envied even the trees
    that could shed their ragged clothes in the autumn
    and sleep indifferent to jobs or an empty belly?

Envying more the tourists moving among the spruce
the peacock Americans riding through resinous woods
the glistening girls in canoes on the cool lakes
For their faces were dustless and blank with ignorance
of tractors or kicks in the rump or three-day hungers
    Something the kid said as we jolted along
    "It's because of them that we're here"
    We squabbled then while the train puffed up the pass
    I called him a red "You can't blame tourists
    They're just lucky that's all; our time will come"

While the heat of the pedal soaks through his boot
this plowman eats old words in the dust
They'll be there again, he thinks, the shining faces
the chosen few who sleep in the summer mountains
eyes innocent now of tanks as then of tractors
and ears unpierced by the whistle of cop or bomb
    But the kid's luck held no farther than Caen

It's not the tourists, he knows, who've robbed him
first of a job and food and then of his brother—
but their lives are consent to all that has been
They live by the throb of this iron in his chest
by the alternation of tractor, boxcar and tank
that others ride and sweat and hunger and die in
while the sleek and their children paddle the glittering rivers
and fish by the friendly fir through a summer's glory
then wing as easy as birds to the soft south
when poplars blazon the long winter's assault

    "You just want what they have" I cracked at the kid
    And so by Christ why not?
    I'd like to see chalets for farmhands
    and the boys who are left of the tank troop
    There's room enough in the mountains
    for them and for tourists
Yet he knows as he turns at the south fence and sees
an oil truck flouring up dust on the section road
    it's not mountains I want nor buddies
    but to feel it won't happen all over again

If the crops from these smoking furrows
the ache in his back, the smile of his wife
were lines in the map of a reasoned future
without booby traps and hidden mortars of class
and the doom forever poised in the world's heaven
then could he sit resolute on this tractor as once in a tank
and the bones of his brother have meaning

And perhaps his moods as he peels the expectant earth
are not so odd to some of his troop
who bore again with agued drills in the damp of mines
or leap to couple treacherous freightcars
or twist the bolts on other tractors for other farmers

but strange no doubt these thoughts of a man on a tractor
to some of the cool tourists
moving on hired ponies under the poised avalanche

Train from Medicine Hat 1945

CANADA: CASE HISTORY: 1945

This is the case of a high-school land,
dead-set in adolescence;
loud treble laughs and sudden fists,
bright cheeks, the gangling presence.
This boy is wonderful at sports
and physically quite healthy;
he's taken to church on Sunday still
and keeps his prurience stealthy.
He doesn't like books, except about bears,
collects new coins and model planes,
and never refuses a dare.
His Uncle spoils him with candy, of course,
yet shouts him down when he talks at table.
You will note he's got some of his French mother's looks,
though he's not so witty and no more stable.
He's really much more like his father and yet
if you say so he'll pull a great face.
He wants to be different from everyone else
and daydreams of winning the global race.
Parents unmarried and living abroad,
relatives keen to bag the estate,
schizophrenia not excluded,
will he learn to grow up before it's too late?

Ottawa

THE EBB BEGINS FROM DREAM

The stars like stranded starfish pale and die
and tinted sands of dawning dry
The ebb begins from dream   leaving a border
of morning papers on the porches

From crusted reefs of homes   from unkempt shores
the workers slip reluctant   half-asleep
lapse back into the city's deep
The waves of factory hands and heads   of salesman
eyes and waiting waitress faces
slide soughing out from night's brief crannies
suck back along the strand of streets
rattling pebbled smalltalk

O then the curves and curls
of girl stenographers
the loops and purls
of children foaming in the ooze
that by the ceaseless moon of living moves
through heaving flats of habit down the day

And late   from tortuous coves   remoter bays
there sets the sinuous undertow
of brokers   and the rolling politicians flow
to welter in the one pelagic motion

Housewives   beached like crabs in staling pools
crisscross   are swashed in search of food
down to the midtown breakers' booming

At last with turning earth   relentless moon
slow but flooding comes the swell once more
with gurge and laughter's plash and murmur
back to the fraying rocks   far-freighted now
with briny flotsam of each morning vow
a wrack of deeds that dulls with neaping
dead thoughts that float again to sea
salt evening weeds that lie
and rot between the cracks of life
and hopes that waterlogged will never link
with land   but will be borne until they sink

Now tide is full and sighing creeps
into the clean sought coigns of sleep
And yet in sleep begins to stir
to mutter in the dark its yearning
and to the round possessive mother turning
dreams of vaster wellings
makes the last cliff totter
cradles all the globe in swaying water

The ebb begins from dream ....

Toronto 1945/Eaglecliff 1947

53

FROM THE HAZEL BOUGH

I met a lady
    on a lazy street
hazel eyes
    and little plush feet

her legs swam by
    like lovely trout
eyes were trees
    where boys leant out

hands in the dark and
    a river side
round breasts rising
    with the finger's tide

she was plump as a finch
    and live as a salmon
gay as silk and
    proud as a Brahmin

we winked when we met
    and laughed when we parted
never took time
    to be brokenhearted

but no man sees
    where the trout lie now
or what leans out
    from the hazel bough

Military Hospital, Toronto 1945/Vancouver 1947

MAN IS A SNOW

Not the cougar leaping to myth
from the orange lynx of our flame
not the timber swooning to death
in the shock of the saw's bright whine
but the rotograved lie
and a nursery of crosses abroad

Not the death of the prairie grass
in the blind wheat's unheeding
but the harvest mildewed in doubt
and the starved in the hour of our hoarding
not the rivers we foul but our blood
o cold and more devious rushing

Man is a snow that cracks
the trees' red resinous arches
and winters the cabined heart
till the chilled nail shrinks in the wall
and pistols the brittle air
till frost like ferns of the world that is lost
unfurls on the darkening window

Elphinstone 1946

ULYSSES

Make no mistake sailor the suitors are here
    and the clouds not yet quiet
Peace the bitchy Queen is back
    but a captive still on shelter diet
The girl of your heart has been knitting long
    the boy-friends have arms there may be a riot
Go canny of course but don't go wrong
    there's no guarantee of an epic ending
Your old dog Time prone on the dungpile
    offers the one last whick of his tail
while you amble by not daring to notice
    and the phony lords grow fat on your ale

Soldier keep your eye on the suitors
    have a talk with your son and the old hired man
but the bow is yours and you must bend it
    or you'll never finish what Homer began

Toronto 1946

DAYBREAK ON LAKE OPAL: HIGH ROCKIES

as
the
fire
from
opals
a trem
-ulous
dawn be-
gins its
ceremony of
s l o w touch
without palms
its breath with-
out breathing along
the whorled turrets
moving shimmering fall
-ing over the scarred for
-ever-by-the-wind-besieged
ramparts the icecracked tree-
breached walls   the light of
the untouchable Sun sliding from
skyblue into the chill broken flesh
of our lifedrop   warming freeing the
silence of jays and firtops   sending a
heather of wind over unfolding asters and
eaglets   ruffling the moated lake to a green
soul and rolling once more the upraised sacrifice
of our world into the sword of Its P R E S E N C E

1946/1970

WINTER SATURDAY

Furred from the farmhouse
like caterpillars from wood
they emerge   the storm blown out
and find in the car their cocoon
Through hardening dusk and over
the cold void impelled they move

to dreams of light and sound
Over drifts like headlands they go
drawn to the town's pink cloud—
gliding unamazed through snow
by the wind marbled and fluted
With tentacle headlights now
they feel the watertank   grope
with Main Street   are blissfully caught
hatch from the car like trembling moths
circle to faces   flutter to movie
throb through the dance in a sultry swoon
But lights fail   time is false
the town was less than its glow
Again in chrysalis folded
they must go lonely
drowsy back through ghosts
the wind starts from the waiting snow

Horseshoe Bay, August 1947

PACIFIC DOOR

Through or over the deathless feud
of the cobra sea and the mongoose wind
you must fare to reach us
Through hiss and throttle come
by a limbo of motion humbled
under cliffs of cloud
and over the shark's blue home
Across the undulations of this slate
long pain and sweating courage chalked
such names as glimmer yet
Drake's crewmen scribbled here their paradise
and dying Bering lost in fog
turned north to mark us off from Asia still
Here cool Cook traced in sudden blood his final bay
and scurvied traders trailed the wakes of yesterday
until the otter rocks were bare
and all the tribal feathers plucked
Here Spaniards and Vancouver's boatmen scrawled
the problem that is ours and yours

that there is no clear Strait of Anian
to lead us easy back to Europe
that men are isled in ocean or in ice
and only joined by long endeavour to be joined
Come then on the waves of desire that well forever
and think no more than you must
of the simple unhuman truth of this emptiness
that down deep below the lowest pulsing of primal cell
tar-dark and still
lie the bleak and forever capacious tombs of the sea

Lowry's "Eridanus," Dollarton 1947

CAN. LIT.
(or *them able leave her ever*)

since we'd always sky about
when we had eagles they flew out
leaving no shadow bigger than wren's
to trouble even our broodiest hens

too busy bridging loneliness
to be alone
we hacked in railway ties
what Emily* etched in bone

we French&English never lost
our civil war
endure it still
a bloody civil bore

the wounded sirened off
no Whitman wanted
it's only by our lack of ghosts
we're haunted

Spanish Banks, Vancouver 1947/1966

*Emily Dickinson

WHAT'S SO BIG ABOUT GREEN?

Something went haywire
about a hundred centuries ago
without Us there to stop it
A tilt?   the icecap melted
saltless water
blocking the gorges
drip & rot all over again

Up from the stinking seas
the corrupt South
slid the fish
The stubborn grass
crept with mice
"Life" was at it again

Our good old lava
made a last try to stop it
boiling up a rash of volcanoes
Still those hydrocarbons
came sloshing back
infecting air/soil/
lakes—like this one

"Opal" they call it—
maybe after the original colour?
"Sulphur" 'd be better
for the springs on the nearshore
still fuming & yellowing up
from the faithful magma
—the one thing that's lasted
holding off even the algae
something pure
perfumed with primal chaos

The first deer must have come in a tremble
to drink at that Lake
noses wrinkling at the stink
Only their taut ears to tell
if a cougar moved in the tree-limbs

Before Us that was
—a few millennia of truce
between leaf, elk & wolf
waterflies, fish & the osprey
a saw-off between berries & birds
& those First Men
the Chehaylis
inching up the outlet stream
to follow sperming salmon

They paddled their dugouts slap into magic
—wounds healed in the springs
when plugged with potash
or the chemistry of belief
So their braves ferried survivors
from tribal wars on the Big River
up to the Lake of Healing
as they called it
& the unwounded waiting round
for the holy water to work
made red oxide doodles on the cliffs
The museums have snaps
taken before We started the quarry
Get-well cards they were maybe
or just "Kilroy was here"

Nobody knows now
The Chehaylis are gone
& the salmon with them
that once blocked the canyons
in a hurry to mate & die

They all went when We came
just a couple of centuries ago
—the whites   the End Men
arrived to set things straight

First the roving Kelts like Fraser
shedding their names
& faiths on the rivers
Then the trappers bypassing Hell's Gate
to build a fort
on the Place of Healing
In ten years they'd cut down the pines
shot off the game & the Indians
caught everything wearing fur
& moved on from the silence they made

But rain & new bush
dissolved the fort
The Lake almost won

1858   We were back
rummaging for gold
On the way north there was time
to cut the trees again
to build & stoke a steamer
ferry mules/camels/horses
& our greatgrandfathers
They rushed up to eat the gold
& died of it

There was another lapse
into a sort of quiet
but nothing's quiet if there's ears
& the slimy chlorophyll's at work
It's our raging Sun
that swims in the real peace
seething away with the Others
unheard & unhearable

In '86 the first train
rumbled through Hell's Gate
A railway really gets
a wilderness by the throat
sends fingers in
to rub the green skin off
This one just tickled the Lake
but it scratched up a fine carcinoma
only two hours away
our grandfathers named Vancouver

They slashed in roads
ran power lines over the balding ridges
sawed the big firs into suburbs
ground small pines into Sunday Supplements
& multiplied that old mephitic stink
into a general sulphite wind

It was our fathers dammed Opal
bit out rock & gravel pits
blasted off the stumps
& hammered up a resort town
Real progress for sure
though no one believed my generation
would be smart enough to finish it

But We were
We straddled the old pool with a highriser
the Place of Healing Chalet
complete with saunas/bars/
resident European psychiatrists
& a heliport on the roof
Copters come in hourly now
rowing ulcerous burghers
from the northamericities
to be dunked in the pool
before colour tv & sedation

Their kids buzz the lakelength
in an hour of speed (on Speed)
drag-racing round the stumps
in the yellow waters
No worry about hitting fisherman
the last mercuric trout
washed bellyupwards long ago
& theres nothing that pullulates
but algae & whatever bugs
live on in oil & shit

No trouble either for the jets
from birds—they went
with the deer & the squirrels

down to the zoos
Some say theres a berrypatch still
at the lake's end
but then some believe in sasquatches
those apemen the Chehaylis saw
on the ridges—Who knows?
You cant see ridges anymore
now that We've got the local overcast
merged with the Continental Permacloud

The peaks are still there
How do We know?   Because the geiger boys
climb up to check the waterfalls
Man they're hotter now than those old springs
but not with sulphur!
Well   so what? the cascades peter out
before they hit the Lake
which We're draining anyway

With the new instant-blasticrete
we can reclaim the bottom
for a new rocketport
then clean off the last greenery
with napalm

So what's so big about green?
It's made to rot
like flesh.   Green   :   gangrene
Bare lava's best
and cousin to the Sun
That's where Life is   genuine Life:
fire and atoms being born
What's happened here on earth
is only science fiction
a nightmare soonest over
Somebody had to get us back
in step with all the other planets

I cant help feeling sort of proud
it's We who've done it
done it all in four generations
made organic death at last
an irreversible reaction
& finished the Original Plan
before 1984

What's more We did it without help
from even one good earthquake
or a new volcano
& without using a single bomb
—just Ourselves
and
      Our kids

Harrison Lake 1949/Aberdeen 1971/Vancouver 1973

TAKKAKAW FALLS

Jupiter   Thor   how he thunders!
High in his own cloud somewhere
smashes
explodes on her upslant ledges
arcs out foaming
falls fighting—
o roaring cold down-geyser—
falls
falls gyring   flings
rain rainbows like peacock flights
vaulting the valley
His own gale rends him
heads off spray-comets
that hurl from her taut cliff
shreds even his cataract core
juggles it
struggles—holds?
falls
ho
like Woden
Zeus
down
terrible the bolt of him
(writhing past firs
foamdrowned to skeletons)
the hissing iced-nebulae whirl of him
crashes
batters unstayable
batters bullthroated
life-lunging

Tak
ka
kaw
batters the brown
throbbing thighs of his mountain

Out of mist meekly the stream

Milk-young he mewls in naked-green moss
bruise-purple boulders
Slickens to slope   pours
silt-turbulent through pine   races
whole to the Yoho   coils
with Columbia   wanders
the ocean tundra   climbs
by sunladders slowly to
storm
glacier
down to the
spawning
thunder

1950

POET-TREE 2

i fear that i shall never make
a poem slippier than a snake
or oozing with as fine a juice
as runs in girls or even spruce
no i wont make not now nor later
pnomes as luverlee as pertaters
trees is made by fauns or satyrs
but only taters make pertaters
& trees is grown by sun from sod
& so are the sods who need a god
but poettrees lack any clue
they just need me   & maybe you

Savary Island 1950/Scarborough College 1966

CLIMBERS

Above the last squeal of wheels
dead-end of the highest road
lithe climbers escape leaping
through fir where chipmunks whirl
Twilight swirls at their backs
magenta hills dissolve
in faces   they curl in crypts
where stone has shelled
and doze while spires snuff out

At dawn along cherry cliffs they stalk
glimpse the peak   on a muskmelon sky
but when glaciers wake chewing
their cud of rock over striped walls
by beryl lakes climbers must shrink
to beetles on brightness   leave birdsong
to follow the spoor of goat over
blocking ramparts by chalky waters

At noon stentorian icefalls call
and hushed they move from the barred old
snow   blindly crawl to cliff's cold
comfort   up up the horny neck of desolation
till their hands bleed at last
from the spines of the crest and they lie
at the end of thrust
weak in weak air and a daze of sight
on the pointless point of the peak

And this is the beginning of space
where there is nothing to say
and no time
except to clamber down down to the road
and the long pigs of the cars squealing

Savary Island 1950

66

BUSHED

He invented a rainbow but lightning struck it
shattered it into the lake-lap of a mountain
so big his mind slowed when he looked at it

Yet he built a shack on the shore
learned to roast porcupine belly and
wore the quills on his hatband

As first he was out with the dawn
whether it yellowed bright as wood-columbine
or was only a fuzzed moth in a flannel of storm
But he found the mountain was clearly alive
sent messages whizzing down every hot morning
boomed proclamations at noon and spread out
a white guard of goat
before falling asleep on its feet at sundown

When he tried his eyes on the lake   ospreys
would fall like valkyries
choosing the cut-throat
He took then to waiting
till the night smoke rose from the boil of the sunset

But the moon carved unknown totems
out of the lakeshore
owls in the beardusky woods derided him
moosehorned cedars circled his swamps and tossed
their antlers up to the stars
then he knew   though the mountain slept   the winds
were shaping its peak to an arrowhead
poised

And now he could only
bar himself in and wait
for the great flint to come singing into his heart

Wreck Beach 1951

THE SPEECH OF THE SALISH CHIEF
(from *The Damnation of Vancouver*)

I have watched, sir, the snow of my people melt
Under the white man's summer.
Where once we hunted, white men have built many longhouses,
But they move uneasy as mice within them.
They have made slaves from waterfalls
And magic from the souls of rocks.
They are stronger than grizzlies.
But their slaves bully them,
And they are chickadees in council.
Some of you say: "Give us time,
We will grow wise, and invent peace."
Others say: "The sun slides into the saltchuk;
We must follow the Redman into the trail of darkness."

Yea, are we not all sons of the same brown Asia tribe?
My fathers, roaming ever eastward,
Crossed Bering, made human half the world.
Your fathers, whitening over Europe,
And ever westering, circled back to us,
Bringing us your woes, clasped in your totems,
Carved in those Powers of lead and steel
We had not known, unknowing had not lacked,
Yet from the knowing needed.

Before the tall ships tossed their shining tools to us
My uncle was our carpenter.
With saw of flame he laid the great cedars low,
Split the sweet-smelling planks with adze of jade,
Bowed them his way with steam and thong,
Shaped the long wind-silvered house
Where fifty of my kin and I lived warm as bear.
He hollowed the great canoes we rode the gulf in, safe as gulls.
My uncle had a Guarding Power with Brother Wood.
Red roots and yellow weeds entwined themselves
Within our women's hands, coiled to those baskets darting
With the grey wave's pattern, or the wings
Of dragonflies, you keep in your great cities now
Within glass boxes. Now they are art, white man's taboo,
But once they held sweet water.

Salmon was bread.
When in the Tide of Thimbleberries
The first silverback threshed in our dipnets
                    My father's drum called all the village.
The red flesh flaked steaming from the ceremonial spit.
My father chanted thanks to the Salmon Power,
and everyone in turn tasted bird-like.
We young men ran to the water.
The bows of our canoes returning were flecked like mica.
With flying fingers the women split the shiny ones,
Hung them on cunning cedar racks,
So that our friends, the air and the sun,
Might seal the good oils for the winter storing.
Salmon was bread.
But there were nights we returned from the mountains
With deer on our shoulders,
Or from the still coves with ducks.
Then all the longhouses made music,
There was roasting of spicy roots,
There were sweet small plums,
The green shoots of vines, and lily bulbs
That grew for us unprompted.
—It was not till *your* time, sir
I saw a Salish go hungry.

There was more, a something—I do not know—
A way of life that died for yours to live.
We gambled with sticks, and storms, and wives, but we
                    did not steal.
  The Chief my father spoke to the people only what was true.
When there was quarrel, he made us unravel it with reason,
      Or wrestle weaponless on the clean sand.
      We kept no longhouses for warriors, we set no state over others.
Each had his work, and all made certain each was fed.
It was a way—

Sometimes a young man would be many months thinking,
Alone in the woods as a heron,
And learning the Powers of the creatures.
When I was young I lay and watched the little grey doctor,
The lizard, I studied his spirit, I found his song.

When I was Chief I carved him on my house-posts.
I took the red earths and the white, and painted his wisdom.
It is true we saw threats and marvels in all that moved,
But we had no god whose blood must be drunk,
Nor a hell for our enemies.
These the white man brought us.

Like dolphin our kindred came, arching over the waves.
My father stood tall on the house-roof,
Threw down soft cloaks of marten and mink,
White rugs of the wild goat's wool,
Tossed down, for the catching, red capes of the cedar bark,
And root-mats brown as the last cloud
In the sun's down-going.
The men made jokes, there was squirrel-chatter of women.
After, at the full tide's brim, they danced,
And my father put on the great-eyed mask of his Power,
With his secret kelp whistle spoke owl-words as he swayed.
My uncle held his drum close to a tide-pool,
Rubbed the skin cunningly with his hands,
Made the downy whoosh of the owl in the night.
A shaman drew frog-talk from cockleshells
Hidden in the pool of his fingers.
The old men sang of the great chiefs that had been,
Their songs dying as wind, then swelling
As the carved rattles clacked,
As the shell-hoops spoke to the ritual sticks…
Once there was silence… no one stirred…
I heard the beat of my heart…
Then like an arrow's thud one beat of the drum, one…
And one… and one… and one
And suddenly all the drums were thunder
And everyone leaped singing and surging in the last dance.…

That was my first potlatch.

In those days we drank only our sounds.
We gave, and we were given to.
But when your fathers took our food and left us
                little coins,
And when your shamans took our songs and left us
                little hymns,

70

The music and the Potlatch stopped.
When the strangers came to build in our village
I had two sons.
One died black and gasping with smallpox.
To the other the trader sold a flintlock.
My son gave the gun's height in otter skins.
He could shoot deer now my arrows fainted to reach.
One day he walked into the new whiskey-house
Your fathers built for us.
He drank its madness, he had the gun,
He killed his cousin, my brother's firstborn...
The strangers choked my son with a rope.
          From that day there was no growing in my nation.
I had a daughter. She died young, and barren
From the secret rot of a sailor's thighs.
When the measles passed from our village
There were ninety to lift into the burial grove.
But the loggers had felled our trees,
There was only the cold earth, and nine men left to dig.
The doctor set fire to the longhouses and the carvings.
My cousins paddled me over the Sound
To sit alone by their smokehouse fire, for I, their Chief, was blind.
One night I felt with shuffling feet the beach-trail.
I walked into the saltwater,
I walked down to the home of the Seal Brother...

Peace to my cousins, comfort and peace.

Vancouver 1952/1957

ELLESMERELAND I

Explorers say that harebells rise
from the cracks of Ellesmereland
and cod swim fat beneath the ice
that grinds its meagre sands
No man is settled on that coast
The harebells are alone
Nor is there talk of making man
from ice cod bell or stone

1952

ELLESMERELAND II

And now in Ellesmereland there sits
a town of twenty men
They guard the floes that reach to the Pole
a hundred leagues and ten
These warders watch the sky watch them
the stricken hills eye both
A mountie visits twice a year
and there is talk of growth

1965

SIX-SIDED SQUARE: ACTOPAN

Do tell me what the ordinary Mex
Madam, there is a plaza in Actopan
where ladies very usual beside most rigid hexagrams
of chili peppers squat this moment
and in Ottomíac gutturals not in Spanish lexicons
gossip while they scratch there in the open

    But arent there towns in Mexico more av—? Dear Madam,
    Actopan is a town more average than mean.
    You may approach it on a sound macadam,
    yet prone upon the plaza's cobbles will be seen
    a brace of ancients, since no edict has forbad them,
    under separate sarapes in a common mescal dream—

        *But someone has to work to make a—*Lady,
        those ladies work at selling hexametric chili,
        and all their husbands, where the zocalo is shady,
        routinely spin in silent willynilly
        lariats from cactus muscles; as they braid they
        hear their normal sons in crimson shorts go shrilly

bouncing an oval basketball about the square—
You mean that all the younger gener—?
I mean this is a saint's day, nothing rare,
a median saint, a medium celebration,
while pigeon-walking down the plaza stair
on tiny heels, from hexahemeric concentration

within the pyramidal church some architect
of Cortés built to tame her antecedents—
You mean that Mexico forgets her histor—? Madam, I suspect
that patterns more complex must have precedence:
she yearns to croon in Harlem dialect
while still her priest to Xipe prays for intercedence.

Actopans all are rounded with the ordinary
and sexed
much as they feel. *You mean—*
they are more hex-
agon and more extraordinary
than even you, dear lady, or than Egypt's queens.

1955

IRAPUATO

For reasons any
                    brigadier
                              could tell
this is a favourite
                    nook
                              for massacre
Toltex by Mixtex Mixtex by Aztex
Aztex by Spanishtex Spanishtex by Mexitex
by Mexitex   by Mexitex   by Texaco   by Pemex

So any farmer can see how the strawberries
are the biggest
                    and reddest
                              in the whole damn continent
but why
                    when arranged
                              under the market flies
do they look like small clotting hearts?

1955

PACHUCAN MINERS

All day in a night of lurch   blast
bend   they have deepened the dark search
their precortesian priests began
into the cold peak's argent
mysteries   Only the ore has risen
into the tasselled wind and run
on singing rails beneath the ardent
sky to sorceries beyond their vision
But now another nugget sun
himself is floated out of thought
and   Orphic and helmeted as divers
are pressed upwards all the miners

Under thin stars by murky troughs
white-eyed they spit   wash rockscurf off
turn without rancour from the guarded gate
below the white Olympus of the gringos
Helmed still and wordless they tramp down
base-metalled roadways to the town
stop where peons by their braziers
shiver to sell them roasted maize
Yet like a defeated army still
descend past blackened walls above
the tree-abandoned valley till
at the lowest street the doors of light

peal out   tequila is a brightness
in the throat   bottles and faces gleam
receive them in a sensible dream
In the cantinas helmets roll
backs fling upright   O now legs are male
are braced   each knotty pair   to hold
up song and hurl it at the night
then step their own way down to where
deep in her torchy den
snakes Toltecan looping in her ears
her crucifix agleam above the sheet
Eurydice lies and hears
the wild guitars   and daily waits
the nightly rescue of her silver men.

Mexico 1955

FRANCISCO TRESGUERRAS*

Half out of your coffin,
Francisco Tresguerras,
you cast a wry look at us,
asking the way.

To the right and the left of you,
off to their Heaven,
their Hell, they go clambering,
all your squat townsmen,

certain of Something,
ignoring your question.
Only you are left clueless,
no man for a queue.

Down here their descendants
avoid still your eye;
black mists of old women
and huddled rancheros
point the nose to the pavement
while round them your columns
rise slender and soaring
into reaches of grace
and trumpets of light.

They have hung up once more
all the clutter you banished;
misshapen pieties
pockmark the sheerness;
mock-blood of a god
drips from your dome.

Yet out of your fresco,
down on the lot of us,
Francisco Tresguerras,
still stares out your face
holding question and answer.
Your Heaven, your Hell is
half out of your coffin
still to be asking,
still the creator,
while the centuries move,
right left and right left,
from the vision arrested,
from the Limbo of art.

Celaya 1955

*Born Celaya, Mexico 1759; died there 1833. Self-taught architect, sculptor, engraver, poet; introduced neo-classical form into the churches of his town, in opposition to the elaborate rococo style prevailing before (and after). One of his churches preserves his *Last Judgement*, containing a self-portrait.

SESTINA FOR THE LADIES OF TEHUÁNTEPEC

"*Teh.* has six claims to fame: its numerous hotsprings
(*radioactive, therapeutic*); moderate earthquakes
(*none in several years*); herbivorous iguanas
(*eaten stewed*); Dictator Porfirio Diaz
(*d. 1911*); its hundred-mile-wide isthmus;
and the commanding beauty of its Indian women."

Stately still and tall as gilliflowers the women
though they no longer glide unwary past the hotsprings
naked as sunlight to each slender softer isthmus
now that ogling busloads (*Greyhound*) make their earth quake
And still skirt-bright before the flaking palace of old Diaz
(*hotel*) they gravely offer up their cold iguanas

Their furtive men (*unfamed*)   who snare iguanas
sliding on tree-limbs olive-smooth as are their women's
have fallen out of peonage to landlord Diaz
into an air more active than their tepid hotsprings
more prompt with tremors than the obsolete earthquakes
rumbling through their intercontinental isthmus

From the stone music of their past the only isthmus
from astronomic shrines fantastic as iguanas
to this unlikely world (*3 bil.*) that waits its earthquake
is their long matriarchal ritual of women
whose eyes from fires more stubborn than under hotsprings
flash out a thousand Mayan years before a Diaz

Goldnecklaced   turbaned   swaying in the square of Diaz
volute and secret as the orchids in their isthmus
braids black and luminous as obsidian by hotsprings
beneath their crowns of fruit   and crested live iguanas
rhythmic and Zapotecan-proud the classic women
dance (*v. marimbas*) their ancient therapy for earthquakes

O dance   and hurl flamboya   till the cobbled earth quakes
let your strong teeth shine out in the plaza lost to Diaz
toss your soaring sunflower plumes   sunflowering women!
Hold for all men yet your supple blossoming isthmus
lest we be noosed   consumed with all iguanas
and leave the radiant leaping of the lonely hotsprings

Beneath all hotsprings lie the triggered earthquakes
Within this grey iguana coils another Diaz
Is there a green isthmus walking yet in women?

Salina Cruz, Mexico 1956

SINALÓA

Si señor, is halligators here, your guidebook say it,
si, jaguar in the montañas, maybe helephants, quién sabe?
You like, dose palmas in the sunset? Certamente very nice,
it happen each night in the guia tourista
But who de hell eat jaguar, halligator, you heat em?
Mira my fren, wat dis town need is muy big breakwater—
      I like take hax to dem jeezly palmas.

So you wan buy machete? Por favor I give you
sousand machetes you give me one grand bulldozer, hey?
Wat dis country is lack, señor, is real good goosin,
is need pinehapple shove hup her bottom
(sure, sure, is bella all dose water-ayacints)
is need drains for sugarcane in dem pitoresco swamps—
      and shoot all dem anarquista egrets.

Hokay, you like bugambilla, ow you say, flower-hung cliffs?
Is ow old, de Fort? Is Colhuan, muy viejo, before Moses, no?
Is for you, señor, take em away, send us helevator for w'eat.
It like me to see all dem fine boxcar stuff full rice,
sugar, flax, rollin down to dose palmstudded ports
were Cortés and all dat crap (you heat history?)—
      and bugger de pink flamingos.

Amigo, we make you present all dem two-wheel hoxcart,
you send em Quebec, were my brudder was learn to be padre—
we take ditchdiggers, tractors, Massey-Arris yes?
Sinalóa want ten sousand mile irrigation canals,
absolutamente. Is fun all dat organ-cactus fence?
Is for de birds, señor, is more better barbwire, verdad?—
      and chingar dose cute little burros.

Sin argumento, my fren, is a beautiful music,
all dem birds. Pero, wy you no like to ear combos,
refrigerator trucks? Is wonderful on straight new ighway,
jampack wit melons, peppers, bananas, tomatoes, si, si . . . .
Chirrimoyas? Mangos? You like! Is for Indios, solamente,
is bruise, no can ship, is no bueno, believe me, señor—
    and defecar on dose goddam guidebook.

Mazatlán, Mexico 1956

MEMORY NO SERVANT

but a stubborn master

Eight years ago   weekend in Veracruz
It was sugary hot   no doubt
I'm sure my bed was a hammock
cocooned in cheesecloth

Oleander?   There must have been...
past the fountains down to the sea
which I rather think was too warm
... or were they hibiscus?
Somebody else recalls that the meals
were good   and cheap
I have some colour slides that surprise me
with improbable cascades
of bugambilla copas de oro

But what I can be sure not to forget:
       Ten feet from the first bridge
       on the highway north from the town
       a turtle coming up from the Gulf
       Both right wheels ran over its middle
       The sound   a crushed carton
       Looking back—
       the untouched head
       ancient   stretched   and still
       moving

Mexico 1956/Ithaca 1963

ALUROID

Blurred in a blot
of laburnum leaves
panther taut
the small Siamese
has willed even her tail's
tip to an Egyptian frieze

But not her two
sapphire burning blue
pools whose planetary bale
to the topmost wren glares through

The silent ritual she brings
they shatter   by their shrill
profanities deny
her lethal godhood
till Bast in anguish springs
her tawny grace at nothing

drops unfelicitous upon
the powermowed lawn
a staring failure
chittering

Dish clinks
and in a breath
she is a fawn
cat   house-intent
Bast's thirty teeth are masked
The terrible fires sink
to almond innocence

The wrens fly off to other deaths

Vancouver 1958

TWENTY-THIRD FLIGHT

Lo as I pause in the alien vale of the airport
fearing ahead the official ambush
a voice languorous and strange as these winds of Oahu
calleth my name and I turn to be quoited in orchids
and amazed with a kiss perfumed and soft as the *lei*
Straight from a travel poster thou steppest
thy arms like mangoes for smoothness
o implausible shepherdess for this one aging sheep
and leadest me through the righteous paths of the Customs
in a mist of my own wild hopes
Yea though I walk through the valley of Immigration
I fear no evil   for thou art a vision beside me
and my name is correctly spelled
and I shall dwell in the Hawaiian Village Hotel
where thy kindred prepareth a table before me
Thou restorest my baggage   and by limousine leadest me
to where I may lie on coral sands by a stream-lined pool

Nay but thou stayest not?
Thou anointest not my naked head with oil?
O shepherdess of Flight Number Twenty-three only
thou hastenest away on thy long brown legs to enchant
thy fellow-members in Local Five of the Greeters' Union
or that favoured professor of Commerce mayhap
who leadeth thee into higher courses in Hotel Management
O nubile goddess of the Kaiser Training Programme
is it possible that tonight my cup runneth not over
and that I shall sit in the still pastures of the lobby
whilst thou leadest another old ram in garlands past me
and   bland as papaya   appearest not to remember me?
And that I shall lie by the waters of Waikiki   and want?

Honolulu 1958

CAPTAIN COOK

The sailor swaggering home to the Yorkshire port
his pouch carved from some unimaginable beast

flashed him a South Sea shilling   Like a javelin
it split the old shop's air
The draper's boy exchanged it from the till
and borrowed a book on navigation

First voyage   mouths burning
from the weevils in the biscuits
charted New Zealand
explored/escaped the Barrier Reef

Second   Antarctica   the bonewhite icefalls

Third   north from the Golden Gate
to where nothing was certain on the maps
except that pike-straight giants' channel
cleaving the continent
from Brobdingnag to Hudson's Bay and home

What they found were kelp-snakes
writhing ship-long on the water
a coast coldly smouldering
Over the drowned peaks heaved the seals
Land was a meaningless tramping of trees
a pikestaffed army pacing them all summer
When it halted   the glaciers took over
The channel invited them up to the polar cap

On the northernest rock
by the keening gulls and the furious emptiness
he left a bottle
with six silver tuppennies George III 1772

Beat back then past Friendly Cove
past wild sweet song from painted mouths
the great birds wooden on the dugout prows
past the white feathers of peace
the glistening cloaks of sea otter

Luffed   endured for that moment when
stumbling shipward through the Hawaiian surf
seeing already the sails run out   belly
and the blue highway stretching sure to Yorkshire
he felt the spear leap through his back
and sank to explore his last reef

Tokyo 1958/York & London 1959

WIND-CHIMES IN
A TEMPLE RUIN

This is the moment
    for two glass leaves
dangling dumb
    from the temple eaves
This is the instant
    when the sly air breathes
and the tremblers touch
    where no man sees
Who is the moving
    or moved is no matter
but the birth of the possible
    song in the rafter
that dies as the wind goes
    nudging other
broken eaves
    for waiting lovers

Nara, Japan 1958

A WALK IN KYOTO

all week   the maid tells me   bowing
her doll's body at my mat   is Boys' Day
also please Mans' Day   and gravely
bends deeper   the magnolia sprig in my alcove
is it male   the old discretions of Zen
were not shaped for my phallic western eye
there is so much discretion
in this small bowed body of an empire
(the wild hair of waterfalls combed straight
in the ricefields   the inn-maid retreating
with the face of a shut flower)   i stand hunched
and clueless   like a castaway in the shoals of my room

when i slide my parchment door to stalk awkward
through lilliput gardens framed & untouchable
as watercolours   the streets look much as everywhere
men are pulled past on the strings
of their engines   the legs of boys
are revolved by a thousand pedals
& all the faces are taut & unfestive as Moscow's
or Toronto's   or mine

Lord Buddha help us all there is vigour enough
in these islands & in all islands reefed & resounding
with cities   but the pitch is high   high as the ping
of cicadas (those small strained motors concealed
in the propped pines by the dying river) & only male
as the stretched falsetto of actors mincing the roles
of kabuki women   or female only as the lost heroes
womanized in the Ladies' Opera—
where in these alleys jammed with competing waves
of signs in two tongues & three scripts
can the simple song of a man be heard?

by the shoguns' palace   the Important Cultural Property
stripped for tiptoeing schoolgirls   i stare
at the staring penned carp that flail
on each others backs to the shrunk pools edge
for the crumb this non-fish tossed
is this the Day's one parable
or under that peeling pagoda the 500 tons
of hermaphrodite Word?

at the inn i prepare to surrender again
my defeated shoes to the bending maid   but suddenly
the closed lotus opens to a smile & she points
to where   over my shoulder   above the sagging tiles
tall in the bare sky & huge as Gulliver
a carp is rising   golden & fighting
thrusting its paper body up from the fist
of a small boy on an empty roof   higher
& higher   into the endless winds of the world

1958

BANGKOK BOY

On the hot
cobbles hoppity
he makes a jig up
this moppet
come alive from chocolate
sudden
with all
small
boys'
joy
dancing under the sun
    that dances
    over the toy king's
    claw roofed palace
    and blazes the roof
    above the latest Hong Kong girlies
    imported to strip
    to the beat of copulation
    and shimmers the broken-china towers
    where ten thousand Buddhas
    sit forever
    on other boys' ashes

In his own time
naked
laughing he
on the scene's edge
like a small monkey-
man
in the endless Ramayana fresco
skips
      that frozen fresco
      of old wars
      under still another glittering Wat
      where tourists worship
      in a regalia
      of cameras
      pacing out their grave
      measures
      along the enormous stone-still
      god
      or splaying
      to immortalize
      the splayed gyrations
      of temple dancers
Beat out
brown smallfry
beat out your own
wild
jive
under this towering strayed
tourist and his bright
strange
cold—whee!—
coin in your small paws
      before in his own motions
      he vanishes
      in the fearful tempo of a taxi
      to that spireless palace
      where god-tall
      in their chalked goblin-faces
      all tourists return
      to plod in pairs like water-buffalo
      by a bare hotel pool
      to their funeral music

Prance
this dazzled instant
of your father's big
Buddha smile
and all the high
world bang in tune
the bright
sun caught
cool
      before in the high world's
      clumpings
      you are caught
      slid lethewards
      on choleric canals
      to where the poles of klongs
      and rows of paddyfields
      are shaped to bend
      small leaping backs
      and the flat bellies
      of impets
      are rounded with beriberi
Scamper little Thai
hot on these hot stones
scat
leap
this is forever O for
all gods' sakes
beat out
that first
last
cry of joy
under the sun!

1958

THE BEAR ON THE DELHI ROAD

Unreal   tall as a myth
by the road the Himalayan bear
is beating the brilliant air
with his crooked arms
About him two men   bare
spindly as locusts   leap

One pulls on a ring
in the great soft nose   His mate
flicks   flicks with a stick
up at the rolling eyes

They have not led him here
down from the fabulous hills
to this bald alien plain
and the clamorous world   to kill
but simply to teach him to dance

They are peaceful both   these spare
men of Kashmir   and the bear
alive is their living   too
If   far on the Delhi way
around him galvanic they dance
it is merely to wear   wear
from his shaggy body the tranced
wish forever to stay
only an ambling bear
four-footed in berries

It is no more joyous for them
in this hot dust to prance
out of reach of the praying claws
sharpened to paw for ants
in the shadows of deodars
It is not easy to free
myth from reality
or rear this fellow up
to lurch   lurch with them
in the tranced dancing of men

Srinagar 1958/Île de Porquerolles 1959

THE SHAPERS: VANCOUVER

1

a hundred million years
for mountains to heave
suffer valleys
the incubus of ice
grow soil-skin

twenty thousand for firs to mass
send living shafts out of the rock

2

with saw of flame
vice of thong
jade axe
the first builders contrived their truce
with sea & hill

out of high cedar slid the longboats
out of sweet wood the windsilvered homes
set tight against the rain's thin fingers
a prose for endurance

out of human fear & joy
came the Shapes beyond lust
the Fin totemic
the incomputible rhythms
the song beyond need

3

set down a century only
for the man on the spar-top
the pelt of pavement
quick thicket of boxes
the petrified phalli
out of the stone

in the screaming chainsaws
we hushed the old dreamers
in the hullabaloo of bulldozers
dynamite dynamo crane dredge combustion
buried them deeper than all compution

walking alone now
in the grandiloquent glitter
we are lost for a way
for a line
bent for the mere eye's pleasure
a form beyond need

is there a rhythm drumming from vision?
shall we tower into art   or ashes?

it is our dreams will decide
& we are their Shapers

Point Grey 1958/Kitsilano 1968

TAVERN BY THE HELLESPONT

What I want is not the flattery
of a second brandy
from the square hand
of this perfunctory Kurd
nor even Alexander's non-coms bodying
from the heavy air of history
If I could bridge their Greek
and they came chattering and dust-red from Asia
to these wharfstones
a tipsy Xenophon in tow
we would sit single
to the radio's jazz

Flailing beyond the swarthy strait
is that isolated light
they call Leander's still
but I'm no Hero
not of either sex
and do not look to see
love swimming naked toward me out of story
nor to be companioned
in a passionate terror
by resonance of bronze
or musket's blatter
beyond those yellow lamps
that peter out
below the solitary stars
to Troy

Is it for a better poet
longer swimmer
that I linger
holding like a cold sea-stone
in this smouldering Byzantium night
my loneliness?

If he should re-emerge
shake his wet arrogance off
sway on a lordly clubfoot
to my table's other chair
what would he stretch me
in the way of friendship
beyond the hand
that carved his unaccompanied name
deep in Poseidon's firmest pillar on Cape Sounion?
"Byron" was here
Duke Humphrey
Haliburton
Childe Kilroy
and are not now

Nor is that singular woman
though she casts such subtle guesses
in her throaty English
that her yoke of forlorn tourists
squeal in soft delight
and think her priestess eyes are doubly real
as television
"We caint keep no secrits from you, ma'am
Ah tail you, yore a spy!"
But what they might reveal
they do not know

Between the individual tables
couples
uncoupled by the radio's decision
turn to their true oneness
which is loneness
and pairing is how it multiplies

To remember this
is all the strength I have
for pacing other swimmers
solo in the uncrossed gulf

Istanbul 1958/Toronto 1974

FIRST TREE FOR FROST

When I was five   before the freeze went deep
my father dug me from the bush a sleeping
spruce   all greenness and limp claws
We planted it beside the gate to grow
with me   Her crown was just below my nose

But all she did that endless winter was
to make herself a cave of snow   and doze
When ground came back I topped her by my lips
In June she seemed to waken at the tips
Just keep it watered   even spruce must drink
my father said   Right through the summer's heat

I lugged jam-bucketsfull and watched my giving sink
down to those feet I could not see
That water was so cold it curled my hands
I felt the needles chilling on my tree
I stole hot kettle water   suds from pans
but those stiff branches never stirred for me
No prayers or heavings   nothing could begin
for all my care   to lift her past my chin

Then the white frosts crept back   I took
to slipping out when no one looked
and poured the steaming crescent of my pee
over the shivering body of my tree
That brown offering seemed to satisfy—
a warm tan mounted to her head

My father never understood   no more than I
why one day suddenly we found it dead
I've let trees go their own way since
Some things my loving never has convinced

Idaho State University 1960

EL GRECO: *ESPOLIO*

The carpenter is intent on the pressure of his hand

on the awl   and the trick of pinpointing his strength
through the awl to the wood   which is tough
He has no effort to spare for despoilings
or to worry if he'll be cut in on the dice
His skill is vital to the scene   and the safety of the state
Anyone can perform the indignities   It's his hard arms
and craft that hold the eyes of the convict's women
There is the problem of getting the holes exact
(in the middle of this elbowing crowd)
and deep enough to hold the spikes
after they've sunk through those bared feet
and inadequate wrists he knows are waiting behind him

93

He doesn't sense perhaps that one of the hands
is held in a curious gesture over him—
giving   or asking   forgiveness?—
but he'd scarcely take time to be puzzled by poses
Criminals come in all sorts
as anyone knows who makes crosses
are as mad or sane as those who decide on their killings
Our one at least has been quiet so far
though they say he talked himself into this trouble
a carpenter's son who got notions of preaching

Well here's a carpenter's son who'll have carpenter sons
God willing   and build what's wanted
temples or tables   mangers or crosses
and shape them decently
working alone in that firm and profound abstraction
which blots out the bawling of rag-snatchers
To construct with hands   knee-weight   braced thigh
keeps the back turned from death

But it's too late now for the other carpenter's boy
to return to this peace before the nails are hammered

Point Grey 1960

VILLANELLE

What shall I do with all my sea
your sun and moon have set alight
till you will swim along with me?

Its day, that lives outlandish free,
the flakes that fall within its night—
what will I do with all my sea?

How long on earth a refugee,
how far from water take the flight
till you have willed to swim with me?

Your room walls off transplendency.
These shores, the rising rocks, are bright—
what may I do with all my sea?

The strong day crumbles on the quay,
the windrows waste across the bight
till you will swim along with me.

I dive alone and grope to see
what salt and tidal things we might
but cannot reach with all our sea
till you have willed to swim with me.

Bowen Island 1961

SIXTH GRADE BIOLOGY QUIZ
(answers supplied by a rat)

To what order do the rats belong?
    To a superior order.
Where do they make their homes?
    In shelters underground
    below your lethal border.
How are their children born?
    From hydrocarbon links like yours
    but harder.
What do they eat?
    Your world's unguarded larder.
Why are they dangerous to human health?
    Because your health is our chief danger.
Have they any use for science?
    Yes, we trust in science, rodent science.
    Beneath your lab, your launching pad, your manger
    we carry on our underground research
    and learn more ways to multiply and wait
    till men have cleared themselves
    and cats
    and left the streets to glare at sky
    and there is freedom to preside
    for rats

Lieben 1961

BILLBOARDS BUILD FREEDOM OF CHOICE
—Courtesy, Oregon Chambers of Commerce—

(billboard on coastal highway)

Yegitit?
Look see
        AMERICA BUILDS BILLBOARDS
so billboards kin bill freedoma choice
between—yeah between billbores no
     WAIT
its yedoan hafta choose no more between
say like trees and billbores lessa course
wenna buncha trees is flattint out inta
       BILLB—
yeah yegotit
youkin pick between well
hey!   see!   like dat!
       ALL VINYL GET WELL DOLLS $6.98
or—watch wasdat comin up?
       PRE PAID CAT?
       PREPAID CATASTROPHE COVERAGE
yeah hell youkin have damnear anythin
       FREE 48 INCH TV IN EVERY ROOM
see!   or   watchit!
       OUR PIES TASTE LIKE MOTHERS
yeah but look bud no chickenin out
because billbores build
       AM—
yeah an AMERICA BUILDS MORE
buildbores to bill more—
sure yugotta! yugotta have
       FREEDOM TO
hey! you doan wannem godam fieldglasses!
theys probly clouds on Mount Raneer
but not on
       MOUNT RAINIER THE BEER THAT CHEERS
and not on good old yella
       SHELL

keepin de windoff yuh from allose clammy beaches
Landscapes is for the birds fella
yegotta choose between well like
between two a de same
hell like de man said Who's got time
for a third tit? *two* parties is *Okay*
that's   DEMOC   sure but yegit three
yegot COMMIES I'm tellinyeh
is like dose damfool niggers in
in Asia someweres all tryin to be nootrul
I tellyeh treesa crowd   a crowda
godamatheisticunamericananti
        BILLBORES
yeah an yewanna help Burma?   help
        BURMA SHAVE
yewanna keep the longhairs from starvin?
        BUY HANDMADE TOY SOLDIERS
yegotta choose fella yegotta
choose between
        AMERICA and UN—
between KEE-RISPIES and KEE-RUMPIES
between KEE-RYEST and KEE-ROOST-SHOVE
and brother if you doan pick
        RIGHT
you better
git this heap
tahelloffn
our
        FREEWAY

1961/1962

NOVEMBER WALK NEAR FALSE CREEK MOUTH

I

The time is the last of warmth
and the fading of brightness
*   before the final flash and the night*

I walk as the earth turns
from its burning father
here on this lowest edge of mortal city
where windows flare on faded flats
and the barren end of the ancient English
    who tippled mead in Alfred's hall
    and took tiffin in lost Lahore
drink now their fouroclock chainstore tea
sighing like old pines as the wind turns

The beat is the small   slap   slapping
of the tide sloping   slipping
its long soft fingers into the tense
joints of the trapped seawall

More ones than twos on the beaches today
strolling   or stranded as nations
woolly mermaids   dazed on beachlogs
a kept dog   sniffing   leading his woman
Seldom the lovers   seldom as reason
They will twine indoors from now to May
or ever to never   except the lovers
of what is not city   the refugees
    from the slow volcano
    the cratered rumbling   sirening vents
    the ashen air   the barren spilling
    compulsive rearing of glassy cliff
    from city
they come to the last innocent warmth
and the fading
before the unimaginable brightness

II

The theme lies in the layers
made and unmade by the nudging   lurching
spiralling down from nothing

down through the common explosion of time
through the chaos of suns
to the high seas of the spinning air
where the shelves form   and re-form down
through cirrus to clouds on cracking peaks
to the terraced woods and the shapeless town
and its dying shapers

The act is the sliding out
to the shifting rotting
folds of the sands that lip
slipping to reefs and sinking cliffs
that ladder down to the ocean's abyss
and farther down through a thousand seas
of the mantling rock
to the dense unbeating black unapproachable
heart of this world

Lanknosed lady sits on a seawall
not alone   she sits with an older book
Who is it?   Shakespeare   Sophocles   Simenon?
They are tranced as sinners unafraid
in the common gaze to pursue
under hard covers their private
affair   though today there is no unbusy body
but me to throw them a public look

    not this wrinkled triad of tourists
    strayed off the trail from the rank zoo
    peering away from irrelevant sea
    seeking a starred sign for the bus-stop
    They dangle plastic totems   a kewpie
    a Hong Kong puzzle for somebody's child
    who waits to be worshipped
    back on the prairie farm

No nor the two manlings
all muscles and snorkels and need to shout
with Canadian voices   Nipponese bodies
racing each other into the chilling waters
last maybe of whatever summer's swimmers

Nor for certain the gamey gaffer
asleep on the bench like a local Buddha
above them   buttonedup mackinaw
Sally Ann trousers   writing in stillness
his own last book   under the squashed
cock of his hat   with a bawdy plot
she never will follow

A tremor only of all his dream
runs like fear from under the hat
through the burned face to twitch
one broken boot   at the other end
of the bench as I pass

dreaming my own unraveled plots
between eating water and eaten shore
      in this hour of the tired and homing
      retired   dissolving
      in the days of the separate wait
      for the mass dying

and I   having clambered down to the last
shelf of the gasping world of lungs
do not know why I too wait   and stare
before descending the final step
into the clouds of the sea

III

The beat beating   is the soft cheek
nudging of the sly   shoving   almost
immortal ocean at work
on the earth's liquidation

Outward the sun   explodes light
like a mild rehearsal of light to come
over the vitreous waters
At this edge of the blast
a young girl sits on a granite bench
so still as if already only
silhouette burned in the stone

Two women pass in a cloud of words
        ... so I said   You're *not*!?
        and she said   I *am*!
        I'm one of the Lockeys!
        Not the Lockeys of *Outgarden* surely
        I said   *Yes* she said   but I live
        in Winnipeg now   Why for heaven's *sake*
        I said   then you *must* know Carl *Thorson*?
        Carl? she said   he's my cousin by marriage
        He *is* I said   why he's *mine* too! So...

Born from the glare come the freakish forms
of tugs   all bows and swollen funnels
straining to harbour in False Creek
and blindly followed by mute scows
        with islets of gravel to thicken the city
        and square bowls of saffron sawdust
        the ground meal of the manstruck forest
or towing shining grids of the trees stricken

At the edge of knowledge the *Prince Apollo*
        (or is it the *Princess Helen*?)
floats in a paperblue fusion of air
gulf   Mykenean islands
and crawls with its freight of flesh
toward the glare and the night waiting
behind the hidden Gate of the Lions

IV

The beat is the slap slip   nudging
as the ledges are made   unmade
by the lurching swaying of all the world
that lies under the spinning air

from the dead centre and the fiery circles
up through the ooze to black liquidities
up to the vast moats
where the doomed whales are swimming
by the weedy walls of sunless Carcassonnes
rising   rising   to the great eels waiting
in salt embrasures   and swirling up
to the twilit roofs that floor the Gulf
up to the crab-scratched sands
of the dappled Banks

into the sunblazed living mud
and the radiant mussels
that armour the rocks

    and I on the path at the high-tide edge
    wandering under the leafless maples
    between the lost salt home
    and the asphalt ledge where carhorns call
    call in the clotting air by a shore
    where shamans never again will sound
    with moon-snail conch the ritual plea
    to brother salmon or vanished seal
    and none ever heard
    the horn of Triton or merman

V

The beat is the bob   dip   dipping
in the small waves   of the ducks shoring
and the shored rocks that seem to move
from turning earth or breathing ocean
in the dazzling slant of the cooling sun

Through piled backyards of the sculptor sea
I climb   over discarded hemlock saurians
     Medusae cedar-stumps   muscled horsemen
     Tartars or Crees   sandsunk forever
and past the raw sawed butt
     telltale with brands
of a buccaneered boom-log
     whisked away to a no-question mill

all the swashing topmost reach of the sea
     that is also the deepest
     reach of wrens   the vanishing squirrel
     and the spilling city
the stinking ledge disputed by barnacles
waiting for tiderise to kick in their food
contested by jittery sandfleas
and hovering gulls that are half-sounds only
traced overhead   lone as my half-thoughts
     wheeling too with persistence of hunger
     or floating on scraps of flotsam

VI

Slowly   scarcely sensed   the beat
has been quickening now as the air
from the whitened peaks is falling
faraway sliding   pouring down
through the higher canyons and over
knolls and roofs to a oneway urgent
procession of rhythms

blowing the haze from False Creek's girders
where now I walk as the waves stream
from my feet to the bay to the far shore
where they lap like dreams that never reach

The tree-barbed tip of Point Grey's lance
has failed again to impale the gone sun
Clouds and islands float together
out from the darkening bandsaw of suburbs
and burn like sodium over the sunset waters

Something   is it only the wind?
above a jungle of harbour masts
is playing paperchase with the persons
of starlings   They sift and fall
stall and soar   turning
          as I too turn   with the need to feel
          once more the yielding of moist sand
          and thread the rocks back to the seawall

shadowed and empty now
of booklost ladies or flickering wrens
and beyond to the Boats for Hire
where a thin old Swede clings in his chair
like hope to the last light

eyeing bluely the girls with rackets
padding back from belated tennis
while herring gulls make civic statues
of three posts on the pier
and all his child-bright boats
heave unwanted to winter sleep

          Further the shore dips   and the sea   sullen
          with sludge from floors of barges   spits
          arrogantly over the Harbour Board's wall
          and only the brutish prow of something
          a troller perhaps   lies longdrowned
          on an Ararat of broken clamshells
          and the flakings of dead crabs

          The shore snouts up again
          spilling beachlogs glossy and dry
          as sloughed snakeskins
          but with sodden immovable hearts
heigh ho the logs that no one wants
and the men that sit on the logs
that no one wants
while the sea repeats what it said
to the first unthinking frogs
and the green wounds of the granite stones

By cold depths and by cliffs
whose shine will pass any moment now
the shore puts an end to my ledge
and I climb past the dried shell
of the children's pool   waiting like faith
for summer   to where the last leaves
of the shore's alders   glistening with salt
have turned the ragged lawns
to a battlefield bright with their bodies

VII

For the time is after the scarring of maples
torn by the fall's first fury of air
on the nearest shelf above brine and sand
where the world of the dry troubling begins

the first days of the vitreous fusing
of deserts   the proud irradiations of air
the clotting oceans
in the years when men rise
and fall   from the moon's ledge

while the moon sends   as before
the waters swirling up and back
from the bay's world
to this darkening bitten shore

I turn to the terraced road
the cold steps to the bland new block
the human-encrusted reefs
that rise here higher than firs or singing
up to aseptic penthouse hillforts
to antennae above the crosses
pylons marching over the peaks
of mountains without Olympus

Higher than clouds and strata of jetstreams
the air-roads wait the two-way traffic
And beyond?   The desert planets
What else?   a galaxy-full perhaps
of suns and penthouses waiting

But still on the highest shelf of ever
washed by the curve of timeless returnings
lies the unreached unreachable nothing
whose winds wash down to the human shores
and slip   shoving

into each thought nudging my footsteps now
as I turn to my brief night's ledge

in the last of warmth
and the fading of brightness
on the sliding edge of the beating sea

Vancouver 1961/Ametlla, Spain 1963

ARRIVALS   Wolfville
Locals
From Halifax   30 Mins. L

It was the hand that caught in me

Sudden as a beast the blizzard
had whirled on us   was gone
as quick over the hill and howling
through the next village   whose spire
could be glimpsed blotting out now
in a grey fury

And we are wading   a straggle of passengers
in town shoes   through a snowscape
clean and cosy as any Christmas card
the small firs like spunwhite candy
spaced on the ice-cream hillocks

Already the sunlight smoulders down
burning on the narrow tracks at the crossing
and fires the sleet that sheathes one flank
and the bland diesel-face of our train
so small and innocent now it has stopped

You wouldn't think from that little jolt we got!
...Speedin... Naw, in that storm he jes couldn see

    Green as a great bruise
    where the smooth flesh of the drifts
    has been savaged   the auto lies
    crumpled and akimbo
    like a beetle battered by catspaw

Flung it fifty feet... Yeah an him further...
This year's chevvy... Well we stopped fast enough

    We stand   the unsilent   stamping
    staring   to reduce to livable size
    what is casually spreadeagled here in the snow

Should be a law about level cross—
Sure but we oughta wistled wen—Hell we did!
...Anybody know who he is?

    We too anonymous   one to the other
    but our breaths write on the air
    the kinship of being alive
    surrounding the perfect stranger

Christ it's too cold I'm gittin back...
Yep ain't nothin we kin do... Hey look
He's only gone three hunderd...

A thin man unprompted is gathering papers
slewed from a briefcase over the raddled banks
He slaps them free of flakes
and packs them carefully back in the case
Now he teeters   not knowing what to do with it
The brakeman plods up with a plaid blanket

Train gonna be held up till police come?
...No I'm stayin
Conductor was up to that farm phonin em

    The man with the case silently lays it
    next to the open palm
    the blanket has failed to cover
    He offers his only remark

Assizes is on up to Wolfville
Them's law papers

    The halfburied engine continues to tick
    with cooling   something live under the snow
    Each time we are startled

Lawyer eh?... Musta stalled on the track
grabbed his case got half out his door...
Yep nearly made it... Young feller too

    The sun has given way again to a black sky
    Most have tramped back to the train
    The rest of us circle about
    as if for somewhere to put down the guilt

Yer all lucky we dint go offa the tracks
... He's right   Can't blame the crew none

    Diesel shrieks and we jump
    The brakeman gestures   Turning at once
    we leave him beating his arms for warmth
    turn in a pleasure of hurry   to hop
    like schoolboys back in the steps we made
    eager for heat and motion   arrivals
    and shaping already what happened

    The train moves to its goal
    and scatters us from the scene forever
    The manner of hills   words   faces
    slides from the gloss protecting each mind
    We will forget even that scotched face perhaps
    waiting till the gay rug came down
    in a Christmas world

    But not surely the longfingered hand
    stretched in some arresting habit of eloquence
    to the last irrational judgement
    roaring in from the storm

    Or is it only in me that the hand hooked
    and I who must manage it now like a third?

Nova Scotia 1962

FOR GEORGE LAMMING

To you
    I can risk words about this

Mastering them   you know
    they are dull
        servants
who say less
    and worse
        than we feel

That party above Kingston Town
    we stood   five (six?) couples

linked singing
    more than rum happy

I was giddy
    from sudden friendship
wanted   undeserved

    black tulip faces

self swaying forgotten

    laughter in dance

Suddenly on a wall mirror
    my face assaulted me
stunned to see itself
    like a white snail
        in the supple dark flowers

Always now I move grateful
    to all of you
who let me walk thoughtless
    and unchallenged
in the gardens
    in the castles
        of your skins*

Off Haiti 1962

In the Castle of My Skin is the title of George Lamming's autobiography of his
childhood as an impoverished black boy in British-colonial Barbados.

CURAÇAO

I think I am going to love it here

I ask the man in the telegraph office
the way to the bank
He locks up and walks along with me
insisting he needs the exercise

When I ask the lady at my hotel desk
what bus to take to the beach
she gets me a lift with her beautiful sister
who is just driving by in a sports job

And already I have thought of something
I want to ask the sister

1962

MEETING OF STRANGERS

"Nice jacket you got dere, man"

He swerved his bicycle toward my curb
to call   then flashed round the corner
a blur in the dusk   of somebody big
redshirted   young   dark   unsmiling

As I stood hoping for a taxi to show
I thought him droll at least
A passing pleasantry?   It was frayed
a sixdollar coat   tropical weight
in this heat only something with pockets
to carry things in

Now all four streets were empty
Dockland   everything shut

It was a sound no bigger than a breath
that made me wheel

He was ten feet away   redshirt
The cycle leant by a post farther off
where an alley came in   What?!

My turning froze him
in the middle of some elaborate stealth
He looked almost comic   splayed
but there was a glitter
under the downheld hand
and something smoked from his eyes

By God if I was going to be stabbed
for my wallet (adrenalin suffused me)
it would have to be done in plain sight
I made a flying leap
to the middle of the crossing
White man   tourist   surrogate   yes
but not guilty enough
to be skewered in the guts for it
without raising all Trinidad first
with shouts   fists   feet   whatever
—I squared round to meet him

and there was a beautiful taxi
lumbering in from a sidestreet
empty!

As I rolled away   safe as Elijah
lucky as Ganymede
there on the curb I'd leaped from
stood that damned cyclist solemnly
shouting

"What did he say?"   I asked the driver
He shrugged at the windshield
"Man dat a crazy boogoo
He soun like he say
'dat a nice jump you got too'"

Port-of-Spain 1962

LETTER TO A CUZCO PRIEST

Father   whose name
your smalltown paper took in vain

Young father   whose face
blurred in the cheap newsprint
I could not recognize in a street

Father   who will never know me
nor read this   which is written
in your honour
in the terms of my worship

Father   forgive yourself

    This morning two Quechuanos
    tramped on their horny feet
    down sun-ravaged slopes
    clutching cardboard banners
    Thirty more Indians followed
    sunfaced   silent   ragged
    and as many boneknobbly goats
    maybe a hundred sheep
    gut-swollen   yammering
    Their dust rose   was carried
    by thin winds like incense
    over sculptured rocks
    that once bore up the Moon's Temple

    Dry wail of the beasts
    dropping over denuded terraces
    enchanted the ears of travellers
    lining up two Cuzco kids
    (dressed like Inca princelings
    by the Oficina de Tourismo)
    to be shot by cameras
    in front of the Bath of the Priestess

Father   worship yourself

> Where stony slopes level
> to unfenced valleys   the sheep
> took over the lead   sniffing grass
> not the boundary stakes

Father you were not with those shepherds
but your Word sent them

> A local watchman for the Lima agent
> for the American banker
> for the Peruvian landowner
> living in Madrid
> phoned the Cuzco cops
> who phoned the army regiment
> quartered locally to handle such jobs

Father   the guilt is not yours
though words that blazed last week
from your pulpit lettered their placards

> The two who bore them are dead

Father   the guilt begins
in the other pulpits and all the places
where no one will say your words

> "The Government is only
> an armed front for Fifty Families"

where no one calls on whatever his country

> "Let the land feed its people"

Father   the guilt is not that you spoke
nor that the poor listened   acted
have come again to defeat

> Twenty of those who followed
> into convenient range of the troops
> tend their own wounds
> in the jail's bullpen

Father   forgive all men if you must
but only in despite of god
and in Man's name

    Their flocks   driven back
    to the spiny heights
    are herded now by the boys and women

Do not forgive your god
who cannot change   being perfect

    Blood dries on the uncropped grass
    The goats eat dust

Father   honour your Man,
though he will not honour you
in whatever priestly purgatory
authority muffles you now

    In Cuzco the paper that quoted the sermon
    and printed your face
    today demands death
    for the Red (Indian?) spies in the Andes

Father   gullible and noble
born to be martyred
and to be the worthy instrument
of the martyrdom of the gullible

    I who am not deceived
    by your cold deity

    believe

    for there is no other belief

    in the wild unquenchable God
    flaming within you

Pray to yourself above all for men like me
that we do not quench
the Man
in each of us

Cuzco, Peru 1962

114

CARIBBEAN KINGDOMS

Flowers live here as easily as air
They hang from power lines   they grow on light
A scalloped leaflet lying on a stair
will puff pink buds   and root itself in stone—
The animal hunts by day or pads within the night

The waxy jasmine   Indian arum   red mimosa
tangle unbruised   thigh to alien thigh
the dark Ashanti Blood   the yellow roses
keep peace beneath a prism sun—
White men alone the rainbow world deny

Stubborn as coral the crimson flowers rise
The torch plant towers higher than a man
Each dawn hibiscus gaze with newmade eyes
and cereus nightly stars the jungle roof—
The other kingdom rules what roosts it can

Petal and bract outdo the stir of sky
Their silent cockatoos in every park
preen and are fed without the need to fly
Coldly they nourish birds of heat   and shelter
all bony forms that cry before the dark

Still souls of butterflies the orchids poise
about the flaming trees and are not singed
Lilies turn spiders into spirit   dragons to toys
The Passion Flower lifts its crucifix unmanned —
Only the worlds of blood on suffering are hinged

When all the life of sound has milled
to silence I think these vines will find
a way to trumpet green and purple still
and jacarandas ring their bells down ruined streets—
Our kingdom comes and goes with mind

Mona, Jamaica 1962

115

TRANSISTOR

She clung to the broom
a long witchy affair she'd been using
to swipe the ancient floor
of the one habitable room
when we came in for a breather
out of the jeep and the humid morning
to this guesthouse
where no one stayed any more
Eyes too bright to be plumbed
gleamed above the homemade handle
She was just tall enough to see over
and her arms   from the grip of the hands
were torsioned as burnt tree-roots

"Like she was hol'in a mike"
the engineer's little black steno said
and giggled   drifting then to the porch
where her boy friend already had vanished
They had come along for the ride

But the old woman was belting songs out
as if she had to send them all the way
back to the sea and the canebrakes
her greatgrandfather ran from
the night he brought her words
stored in his rebellious head
beyond the howl of the slavers' hounds
to this remotest hilltop in Jamaica

In truth she'd never faced mike nor tape
Today was the first she'd seen a transistor
and she'd stared at that more with fear
than interest when the little steno
had sauntered by from the jeep with it

An anchor to keep the rest of her tiny self
from floating up level with the notes
was more what she needed the broom for
I thought   utterly stilled in my chair
under the clean power
coiled in four generations of skulls
and springing out now
from the mouth of this bird-still body

It was the engineer she sang for
because he had asked her
he always did
Yet mine was a new face
with the colour to make anyone wary
up in these mountains
So she stood poised for reversal
back to the caretaker's role

But she soon forgot me   him too
as her mind unravelled to airs
a grandmother might have woven
stooping in dappled coffee groves
when this was a plantation house
buzzing with whiteman's prospering

She paused only once   to down a glass
the engineer poured from the rum he'd brought
He knew what songs to ask for
and out they came now whorling
as if her voice were immortal and separate
within her   and she only the toughened reed
vibrated still by the singing dead
by the slaved and the half-free
The narrow high-ceilinged room was a box
resounding with all the mourning of loves
and deaths   the fear of Mamba   hope of Jesus
the bitter years and the bawdy
till suddenly   at her first falter
she seemed to listen
and stopped

It was not quite all
though my thanks alone might have sent her off
if the engineer hadn't silently offered
a second rum   The besom again in one hand
like a rifle at ease
she swung to me
and in the grave high rhythms of the Victorians
toasted my health
and that of all the gentlemen of my nation
with all the dignity of hers
then disappeared into her kitchen
broom already waggling

It was only then I let my ear tell me
there'd been a counter-bass going all along
Out on the dusty porch I found the young pair
sitting on the rail at the farthest corner
Two faces black and anxious
leant together under the transistor
They'd found a nail in a pillar to hang it by
The morning disc spin from Puerto Rico
was sending a Hollywood cowboy
from last year's Parade
The machine swung his voice from shriek
to silence and back
I suppose they'd been listening to him
as exclusively as I to her
and out of just as much need
to exchange our pasts

Yallahs Mountain 1962

TORONTO BOARD OF TRADE GOES ABROAD

George! I dunno how you *do* it George...

Wy, eat all at *stuff,* all at horses *doovers* after all we had for *lunch!* I bet
you dunno wat half it *is! Raw fish* fer gossake I betitis you wanna *watch*
that stuff George. Fellah in *Mexico* told me theres *worms* in it...

Gossake George I wish I had your *appetite* I cant *eat* I cant eat *any*thin...

Naw *I'm* not worryin... *Crisis?!*   Hell George I *never* got the wind up and you know *wy* George? Because I allus *knew* that sonfabitch *Kroo*shef had no *guts*...

Naw George its I gotta terrible *thirst.* Its them uh Pis—? Them...

Yeah *Pisscoes! Thats* wot they give us at lunch, yeah *hell* I thought they was kinda mild mar*teen*ies but theyre straight *al*cohol George—an an re*distilled! Wow!*...

Four a them...

Yeah, so wat wouldn I give *now* for, for you know *wat* George? For jus, jus a liddle drink of *water* because you know somethin George? George? This the *longest bar* ina *world*...

Well I bet in Southa Merica anyway...

You take a *look,* hunderd twenny five *mee*tres fellah over there told me, blongsta Club, wy thas—how much *is* that George?

Yeah well thasa lot eh? an George every *yard* of its *piled* with *licker* analla this greazer *chow* yer eatin and you jes try find a drinka *water* on it!...

O sure sure but how you gonna trustim? They doenoe *in*glish George these waiters. Anyway watta *they* care if its contaminated maybe *loaded* with you know *wat* George, wat *you* got in Peroo George!

Well now doan get me *wrong* I wouldn let *them* hear me I'm not criticizin hell *no* these things doan really *matter* itsa great *country* and we all got somethin in *common* Canadians Chileans because you know *wot?* you know wattis we got in common? we're all *Ameri*cans thas wat eh George? thas watta tellem but jussa same George I'd—George I'd give ten *bucks* this *minute* for *one glass* of good old *Lake Ontario tap*water thas wat—George?... George?!

Now where the hell did *he* git to?

Union Club, Santiago de Chile, October 1962

119

CARTAGENA DE INDIAS, 1962

Ciudad triste, ayer reina de la mar
    (Heredia)

Each face its own phantom
its own formula of breed and shade
but all the eyes accuse me back and say

    There are only two races here:
    we human citizens
    who are poor but have things to sell
    and you   from outer space
    unseasonable   our one tourist
    but plainly able to buy

This arthritic street
where Drake's men and Cole's ran
swung cutlasses   where wine and sweet blood
snaked in the cobble's joints
    leaps now in a sennet of taxi horns
    to betray my invasion
All watch my first retreat
to barbizans patched from Morgan's grapeshot
and they rush me
    three desperate tarantula youths
waving Old Golds unexcised

By an altar blackened
where the Indian silver was scratched away
in sanctuary leaning   on lush cool marble
    I am hemmed by a conga drum-man in jeans
    He bares a brace of Swiss watches
    whispers in husky Texan

Where gems and indigo were sorted
    in shouting arcades
    I am deftly shortchanged
and slink to the trees that lean
and flower tall in the Plaza
    nine shoeboys wham their boxes
    slap at my newshined feet

Only in the Indio market
mazed on the sodden quais
I am granted uneasy truce
Around the ritual braidings of hair
the magical arrangements of fish
the piled rainbows of rotting fruit
I cast a shadow of silence
    blue-dreaded eyes
    corpse face
    hidalgo clothes
    tall one   tall as a demon
    pass O pass us quickly

Behind me the bright blaze of patois
    leaps again

I step to the beautiful slave-built bridge
and a mestiza girl
    levels Christ's hands at me
    under a dangling goiter

Past the glazed-eyed screamers of *dulces*
swing to a pink lane
where a poxed and slit-eyed savage
    pouts an obscenity
    offering a sister
    as he would spit me
    a dart from a blowpipe

Somewhere there must be another bridge
from my stupid wish
to their human acceptance
but what can I offer—
my tongue half-locked in the cell
of its language —other than pesos
    to these old crones of thirty
    whose young sink in pellagra
    as I clump unmaimed
    in the bright shoes
    that keep me from hookworm
    lockjaw and snakebite

It's written in the cut of my glasses
I've a hotelroom all to myself
with a fan   and a box of Vitamin C
It can be measured
in my unnatural stride
that my life expectation
is more than forty
especially now that I'm close to sixty

older than ever bankrupt Bolívar was
who sits now in a frozen prance
high over the coconut trays
quivering on the heads
      of three gaunt mulatto ladies
      circling in a pavane of commerce
      down upon spotlit me

Out of the heaving womb of independence
Bolívar rode   and over the bloody afterbirth
into coffee and standard oil
      from inquisitional baroque
      to armed forces corbusier

      He alone has nothing more
      to sell me

I come routed now   scuffling
through dust in a nameless square
treeless burning deserted
come lost and guiltily wakeful
in the hour of siesta
      at last to a message

      to a pair of shoes
      in a circle of baked mud
      worn   out of shape   one on its side
For a second I am shaken by panic
heat? humidity? something has got me
      the shoes are concrete
      and ten feet long

the sight of a plaque calms
without telling me much

En homenaje de la memoria de
LUIS LOPEZ
se erigió este monumento
a los zapatos viejos
el día 10 de febrero de 1957

Luis Lopez? Monument to his old shoes?
What??? There was nothing else
and the square was asleep

Back through the huckster streets
the sad taxi men still begging with horns
to the one bookstore

Si señor   Luis Lopez el poeta
Here is his book
Unamuno praised it   *si si*
You have seen *los zapatos?*   Ah?
But they are us, *señor*
It was about us he wrote
about Cartagena where he was born
and died   See here this sonnet
always he said hard things about us
Said we were lazy except to make noise
and we only shout to get money
ugly too, backward ... why not?
it is for a poet to say these things
Also he said *plena* —how say it?—
plena de rancio desaliño
Full of rancid disarray!
Si, Si, but look at the end, when old
he come to say one nice thing
only one ever about us
He say we inspire that love a man has
for his old shoes—*entonces*
we give him a monument to the shoes

I bought the book   walked back
sat on the curb happier than Wordsworth
gazing away at his daffodils

Discarded queen   I thought   I love you too
Full of rancid disarray
city like any city
full of the stench of human indignity
and disarray of the human proportion
full of the noisy always poor
and the precocious dying
stinking with fear   the stale of ignorance
I love you first for giving birth
to Luis Lopez   suffering him
honouring him at last
in the grand laconic manner
he taught you

—and him I envy
I who am seldom read by my townsmen

Descendants of pirates   grandees
galleyslaves and cannibals
I love the whole starved cheating
poetry-reading lot of you   most of all
for throwing me the shoes of deadman Luis
to walk me back into your brotherhood

Colombia 1962/Greece 1963

PLAZA DE LA INQUISICIÓN

A spider's body
limp and hairy
appeared at the bottom of my coffee

The waiter being Castilian
said passionately nothing
And why indeed should apologies
be made to me

It was I who was looking in
at the spider
It might be years
before I slipped and drowned
in somebody else's cup

Madrid 1963

EPIDAURUS

Taking the baths for their nerves
anxious Corinthian ladies
no doubt complained to the attendants
about the noise
          pedlars

                              MUSSELLLS!
                              FIGgggs!

            donkeys
            foot pilgrims
            weekend chariots
all that shoving and braying
past Aesculapius' own temple
into the great new eyesore of a showplace
and the brawling out again
with torches into the night

Now everything's been put right
                  "the visitor is offered
                  every convenience   easy access
                  unlimited parking   refreshments
                  at the   Tourist Pavilion
                  also a quick & comfortable
                  getaway"
and the season lasts only six weeks

After twenty-five centuries
something is also being done
about the wildflowers
flagrantly widening the cracks
in even the best seats

Everybody however
still waits to
hear the
pin
dr
o

p

Greece 1963

LOOKING FROM OREGON

"And what it watches is not our wars"
          (Robinson Jeffers)

Far out as I can see
into the crazy dance of light
there are cormorants like little black eyebrows
wriggling and drooping
          but the eye is out of all proportion

Nearer   just beyond the roiling surf
salmon   the young or the sperm-heavy
are being overtaken by bird's neb
sealion's teeth   fisherman's talon

The spent waters
          flecks in this corner of the eyeball
falling past my friend and his two sons
          where they straddle the groin's head
collapse on the beach
          after the long race
from where?   perhaps from Tonkin's gulf
          on the bloodshot edge

There's no good my searching the horizon
          I'm one of those another poet* saw
          sitting beside our other ocean
I can't look farther out or in

Yet up here in the wild parsnips and the wind
I know the earth is not holding
tumbles in body-lengths
towards thunderheads and unimaginable Asia

though below me on the frothy rocks
my friend and his two boys
do not look up from fishing

Florence, Oregon, August 1964

*v. Robert Frost's "Neither out Far nor in Deep."

OIL REFINERY

Under the fume   of the first dragons
those spellbinders who guard   goldhoards under barrows
whole fields of warriors   wilted: even Beowulf
fell in balebreath   from firedrake fangs

Yet this hugest of Worms   though he outburst heaving
from deepest of meres   under farthest moor
is led leaping and leaping   at last to these shores
and hour by hour   overhewn and whelmed

Not without fury resists   flames in the night
blasts the world air   wans all blue day
Ho! a handful of thanes   in helmets threaten him
in silver keeps stab him   the old swartshiner
with gauges bedevil   with dials with cyclonesnuffers
endless they slaughter   that slimiest of Nadders

Hwaet! he is quick again   thousand-toothed Queller
whirls his ghost in our wheels   unleashes or locks them
Yea he twins twentyfold   twines in our graveloot
breath of that sly snake   stifles and clings
slides from our long ships   coils round our steadings
Eala! we are lost   in the spell of his loopings.

Port Moody 1964

WAY TO THE WEST

11 pm & sunset still going on
but that could be the latitude
whats wrongs the colour
everywhere horseshit ochre & roiling
like paper that twists/browns
before firing up on hot ashes
theres somebodys hell ahead
meantime our lips prick
& the trees are dead

but its another 20 miles before the sign
        You Are Entering
        SUDBURY
    Home of the world's largest
& christ there on the skull of a hill
3 manhattan-high stacks   a phallic calvary
ejaculating some essence of rotten semen
straight up like mass sabotage at cape kennedy

the damned are all over   the young
shrieking (looking much like anyone)
drag-race with radios up
from one smouldering stoplight to another—
under neon the older faces
assembled from half europe
screwcheeked/pitted all the same way
have something dignified about their devilship
that stares us down   till they come human
& houck brown on the cement

    WELCOME TO . . .   73% OF THE FREE
    WORLD'S NICKEL IS CREATED HERE
& the free world invented a special cough
not even 100 taverns can dampen
nor all the jukes drown in the doorways
of pandemonium   milton thou shouldst
be living etc

DEAD END   wheres west?   sunset folded
our headlights finger dumped cans
wriggle through streets like crevasses
blasted in bedrock pink & folded
like glazed guts on a butchers marble

out of the starless dark falls the roar
of golgotha   how long before one stops
noticing?   & the sting in the eyes?

by a raped old car an indian sits
praying?   puking
            You Are Leaving
            SUDBURY
         Centre of Free Enterprise
& 20 more miles of battlefield

at last a moon looms up
we are into the dumb firs again
      TURN OUT   300 YDS
            HISTORIC SITE
            FRENCH RIVER
what?   canoe route the Hurons found
& showed the whites—
the way to the west   silks   buffalo
vietnam   the moon
shines over the middle of nowhere—
dumb as the trees

we stop for a leak   silence
too late for other cars
the trees listen back
nothing   the owls dead too?

suddenly some kind of low growl
coming up!   we head for the car—
only a night jet

but after it passes we realize
we'd been hearing the river all along

Northern Ontario 1965

THE MAMMOTH CORRIDORS

*From Vancouver, Canada's Pacific metropolis, the
tourist may drive east over the smooth Trans-Canada
Hiway through a*

Turning from the great islands drowning
in the morning's waves from Asia
my car heads me from the city's April
    cherry petals on the slick streets
    against the flayed mountains the billboards
    conjuring perfection   Tahiti
    orgasms of power   death insurance

> *thousand miles of towering Rockies to the prairies.
> Crossing from the north shore at the spectacular
> Lion's Gate, the motorist begins to trace in reverse*

Over the taut bridge   through the lonely park
my wheels will themselves to the shrieking

> *the spectacular route taken by the first explorers
> and hardy traders. Stanley Park, with its convenient
> thruway, aquarium, totem poles (exact replicas of
> originals now stored for preservation) . . . a thousand
> acres of playground where Indians once camped . . .*

Around the highrisers   the sullen leisured
dogs   and the rolling realtors
Then the spastic traffic
of buyers and bought   pedlars of weed and soap
of acid and snow   of work and wonder
'as the world asketh'   in Skidroad's lanes

> *Blessed with relaxing airs, Canada's third
> largest city offers . . . yacht basins, beaches,
> . . . panoramic view, where a modest cairn com-
> memorates . . . British navy in 1729 . . . possession
> of the North Pacific coast from the Spaniards
> who first came to trade with the natives . . .*

Eastward an hour and the master I own
has rushed me to winter and wildness
and merely the grey road coiling and diminishing
upward like a dragon's tail swinges me off
from the unsupportable Real

the tortured peaks
only a breath more broken
the blind dive of the canyons
a scratch of a century deeper
since those first compulsive whites
the Searchers
for gold   absolution   furs   Asia
for a name   death   or mere difference
came hurtling in improbable canoes
heavy with liquor and fear
bearing their beads and syphilis
muzzleloaders and god

According to recent scientific theories, this
was the route taken by the earliest Indians,
at the end of the last Ice Age.

but from the truths that compel me
up the land's one nerve like a virus
to undo in a single day my father's lifetime
of westering
from my own lusts and neckties and novels
from ulcers   vitamins   bulletins   *accidia*
i lie unshielded under each motel's roof

Convenient to transcontinental railroads and a
four-lane hiway . . . offers American visitors every
modern . . . angler's paradise   big game . . .

under the uncontrollable cliffs and the starlight
falling on the same ice-bitten ranges
the first men saw

Having crossed from Asia to Alaska, and followed
the mammoths down corridors in the melting ice-cap,
these earliest Canadians are thought to have reached
a dead-end in their progress south, and been forced
to turn west from the Albertan plains into the Rockies
and so eventually came to the Pacific.

in that century the Siberians took   or more
(and took a hundred centuries ago)
to move by floes and hunger past the point
of no return   trailing the great woolly ones

watching for the gleam of nine-foot tusks
tracking   floundering in the newborn earth
wolving by the black rivers that rattled
from the glare of the narrowing icewalls
till the last red fountains
(*Mammuthus parelephas columbi*   his blood)
gushed on the boggy tundra
at the blind corridor's end

In the nearby museum, mounted specimens of
the wild life,

Surviving westward then over howling summits
the Siberians possessed these still fresh-hewn alps
(which i inheriting do not possess)
    They moved by day through bear and elk
    and by their killing
outliving sleep by capturing the deer's Wit
the Power of cougar
    in nets of dance and word
    the medicine of mask
    the threat of drum

and a spacious diorama outlining the story of
man. No charge.

Three mornings now from the applefoam
and the seas my Engine unreels me
out from the last gouged hills
like a bull straightens
into the prairie's arena
charges in a dazzle of snow the human mesh

Through Calgary, where the Blackfoot trail
once crossed, a four-lane artery helps speed
the traffic of Canada's greatest car-per-capita
city ... in Bowness Park, life-sized models of
dinosaurs that once roamed the area

where all began for me
though the log cabin where first i was forced
into air
is a lost ghost under a vanished bridge
by a dying river

In 1912 Stampede Day was inaugurated to perpetuate
the finest traditions of the pioneer and cowpuncher . . .
now a week of parades, racing, rodeos, and other

An ash of ice whines at the cross of streets
A morning drunk is spattering curses
over a halfbreed girl in a blotched doorway

picturesque events . . . for the traveller from
the west, Calgary is the beginning of the
great Canadian prairie, which though largely
treeless, contains some of the world's richest
wheat-farms and oil deposits . . .

Far and far to the east again
i am pulled to a sky of land
flattened white to the Pole
i am drawn against the unstillable winds
    the breath of that madcap virgin
    mother of ice
    who embraced it all
    a wink ago in the world's eye
    till the sun won us again
    with his roving glance
    and sent her shrinking and weeping
    frozen lakes over the upstart grass

To the north, however, the rich postglacial
soil eventually gives place to tundra, perma-
frost and Arctic conditions . . .

Hoarding her cold passion she lies
the Greenland lodger
and the land's long face   and mine
cannot forget   is graved
with her monstrous rutting
Her time is our secret clock
She waits for all to slow
Then to lust back
wider than Europe and Pacific deep
    bringing her love   the rounded silence
      a long hard peace

1965/1972

IN PURDY'S AMELIASBURG
(first visit 1965)

But Al   this round pond man—
        where's Roblin Lake   I mean the real one?
        where's that great omphalos I know
        corpsegrey below apocalyptic skies?
    this cosy girl's-belly-button
    brims with rosewater
    from one of those frilly May sunsets

Dont get me wrong   I'm grateful to be here
    after Toronto
        still hairy from a long winter
    after Trenton
        that raped that hustled town
it's good here it's peace the blackbirds
are setting off their own springs in the air
    but the air's too bright
it could be I've come the wrong time
    too soon for those horsecrap-fattened peonies
    you reddened the shores with
    too late for skulldeep snow
    stubborn in the fence zags
man there's only dandelions
barring the way to the privy

But no what's wrong is place as well
it's anybody's church across the lake
    the spire shrank
    and that carpenter who fixed it once
    against the sky is off in Trenton
    banging thumbnails and wallboard
    is you in fact
and you're not here   your mouse is hiding
quote representative of an equally powerful race unquote
that heron   the cosmic crying rays
    where in Roblin are they?

In this Ameliasburg a backyard of stones
is where they trucked off Roblin Mill
    declared historical enough
    for reassembly in Toronto
by god they'll whisk your own shack away
if you dont stop writing
    (and Eurithe too the ferocious wife)
    and the very cowpads before your eyes

Al I think they have
I think Somebody's cleaned up
    after your picknicking glaciers
they've raised the roof on the shack
    ringed it with Summer Homes
    told Ptolemy to leave town
    made your spouse patient and young again
it's the Same People of course
    who took the wolves away
    from Malcolm Lowry's woods
    sent Eliot's London Bridge to Arizona
    smoothed Jeffers' headlands back
    into Californian hills
so though it's fine here of course
    it's not Ameliasburg

But wait
    what's popping up when I sweep the kitchen?
        half an envelope
        with half a poem scribbled
and from behind the battered wood-heater
        yet another empty bottle
        smelling absolutely of wild grape

Next morning I drift down a nebulous way
        to the village hardware
        like a madman's tiny museum
        Can-opener   yep   got one
        got one all right   You in a hurry?
        yeah   got mislaid some time back
        I'd have to look   drop in nex week mebbe

I return under the ancient clouds
        the Lake is hazy   endless
what bird is flapping away?
the shack's doorknob turns planetary in my hand—
        Al that's your mouse on the floor bowing!

TO SWINDON FROM LONDON BY BRITRAIL
ALOUD/BAGATELLE

BOOOooooottttttt!
Brrm   brrbb   brrrurn   brrubb
brrrmbl   brrubl   brrrurnmble brumble
brrrumble de bum   brumble de *bug*
drumble le *dug*   droomble de dag
drumbledee dug   drumbledee dag
droobedydag   roobeddy dig
roobity bad   rootilly bittle
roobity bag   rubbity bottle
brrrubeddiddy rash crash crubberrydrubbery crosh
croshoverrails   Sroch   hurry along
hurryalong hurryalane hurryaloon hurryalung
along alane along alung a-law-ing a-law-ing a-laying
adawdle   alane   a dawdel along
agoggle along   a doggle de dung de
dawdillee doggillee   goggillee *gog*
hungary dungaree mongrely dong
mangletree anglesea mingle de   BOOooooottt! Boot!
hungary *dung*   hunger me lung
ganger de lag gagger de lack gangerlag gagerlak
gangerlag gugelak   lagaback loveaduck
look at duck look at lake look at duck
lucky duck   look at drake   look at   whooooosh!
izzza brisssss   is a bridge!
gurrrdee *up*   durridee *down*   diddle de *grrp*
de doodle de dup   de diddle de dee BOOOOO!
de diddle de   BLAST   pasht pasht pasht
pasht past   past   train past de diddle de dip
de griddle de green   de girdle de grin
lay & a lass   lay & a lad
day & dad & hay & gad & may & mad & say & sad

FF staccato
P lento Ped.
poco a poco
accel. e cresc.
Ped. ad lib.
MF stretto
allegretto
F
rapido
FF
F molto rapido

MF allegro
piu rall.
andante
MP tempo di valse

F——FFF brill.
F a tempo
accel.

MF vivace
accel.
F agitato
poco ritard.
con grazia——FF
energico presto
sforz.
leggiero
adagio
delicatissimo

dolce	hay & a mow hay & a cow
PF agit.	cow & moos &——crash! clattr krradge——& cows
FF strepitoso	crashes & ashes & cows ashes & cow——WUNDRRR RR
molto agitato	RRRAILERER THUNder & ragerr blundrrm gauge
F a tempo	gagelak gugelak gagelak gugelag
FF subito con brio	gagelllOOVer passOOver passover pastdover
MF rall.	gagelak gugelak gagelak fugaluck
a tempo	fugadug fulderol fuldedoodle dedoodum
	dedundr passundrr dedunderry boom
cantabile	de bol de rol de boddle le dcl
ma non troppo	de puddle de pill de rodd.e de rill
allegro assai	bottle a pole battle a post buttery post
	frettering peace feathering feast
P calando	pheasanty woods pleasanty words
appassionato	clattering works blathering jerks
espressivo	watery dirt dirtery what
capriccio	waddery turds dirrery waw dirry whaw dirr whee
	woof wee whee with the trees withery twees
PF legato sub. agit.	teas and trees an this an leaves an SQUOO! squaw!
MF moderato	gagelak gugelak gagerack pain pay in the train
risoluto e rall.	bag baggity baggity kroom baggy crude ba koo
ben marcato	koo its a groom doom an a fox dog fox
	fox fox its a fox dog dog dogelak grog
MF grave	grogelak grief grainalack grey
PF sostenuto	gag e lak gud e lak gag a KUNG...KUNG
decresc.	guh delhi de dung de daddle deee
FFF molto sost.	SQUEEEEEEEEK K!——
Con una certa espressione parlante	The tren neow stendinnng on pletfoam thureee is foh Suh——weeeezeen——dawn.

1965/1973

HOKKAI IN THE DEW LINE SNOWS

to sleep under real
stars   wake in the pupil of
original Sun

goodmornings with birds
love naked by waterfalls
o best planet—   whoooM!

a north door opens
the leaves scurry to hole &
the Cat prowls our world

Trumansburg, NY 1966

1984 MINUS 17 & COUNTING AT U OF WATERLOO ONTARIO

after the calorestimated meal
in the male hall
they walk back to the compulibratories
keeping to the asphalt paths
conceived by the landtects

sometimes a thousand are in forward motion
engimechs the plureality   at 0826 hrs
in pairs   with crewcuts   hands by flanks
& slightly crooked below rainbreakers (yellow)
with *U of W* on the back
ENGINEERS on upper sleeve L
& black number upper R

since none of this is actually required by deans
nor the gloves (black)   hushpuppies (grey)
nor absence of headcover & expression
what is felt is communiternity   a campustalt

the mathamen   cruts not quite so short
are sometimes grouped in 3s
but otherwise all waterloobed:
hands by flanks & slightly…(yellow)…
MATHS on…black…grey…absence
almost as striking—communalove at least

a few artsies yet (terminal class of '71)
midearburns / 1 in 10
dress as above of course
but some have briefcases in R hand
wear their ARTS upon their sleeves
& walk alone

1967

CHARITÉ, ESPÉRANCE ET FOI
(a tender tale from early ca-nada)

Once there were 3 little Indian girls
Champlain adopted them from the Montagnais
to show King Louis & the Cardinal it was possible
to make Christian Ladies out of savages
He baptized them Foi (11) Espérance (12) et Charité (15)
then put them in a fort to learn their French

Little Faith wriggled away & split for the woods
but Hope & Charity quickly mastered irregular verbs
& sewing   developed bosoms   went on to embroidery
When Champlain saw they had acquired piety & table manners
he dressed them in style & sailed downstream to Tadoussac
en route to the French Court with Espérance et Charité

But a wicked merchant named Nicolas Marsolet of Tadoussac
got Espérance aside & told her she was what he had to have
She said she had a date in France with King & God
Nick snarled he could have her & her sister given back
to the Indians   & grabbed her round her corset
She pulled a knife & got away to Charité

Les deux étudiantes then wrote Nicholas a letter
Hope began it:
    "Monsieur Marsolet, it was an honour & a pleasure to
    meet you, & I look forward to our next rencontre.
    In anticipation I have sharpened my knife so that
    I may on that occasion give myself the added joy
    of cutting out your heart"
& Charity added:
    "It will give me, monsieur, great pleasure
    to help my sister eat it."
All this sounded more elegant in the original of course
because that was in correct seventeenth-century French

They showed their letter to Champlain
He was impressed   no mistakes in tenses
He told them he was proud they had stood firm
especially against that méchant marchand Marsolet
who ate meat both Fridays & Saturdays   an Anglophile
& sold hooch to their cousin Indians in Tadoussac
However   Champlain added   he didnt think
that Espérance et Charité were ready yet for France

The two young ladies wept   unrolled their broderie
Champlain agreed they were bien civilisées
They went down on their knees   showed him their petticoats
Champlain was kind   admired the sewing   but was firm
It was France   he said   that wasnt ready yet for them
He gave them each a wooden rosary
& sent them back to Quebec with Guillaume Couillard

Couillard was a respectable churchwarden & crop inspector
no merchant   he couldnt read & had 10 children of his own
He was the first to use the plough in Canada

but when Champlain got back from France nobody knew
where Hope & Charity had got to
or if they ever found their Faith again

Montreal 1967

SONG FOR SUNSETS

goodnite sun
im turning over again
im on the little ball
so slowly rolling
backwards from you

i hope youre there
central & responsible
burning away
all thru the black
of my dumb
somersault

i'll tumble around
& wake to you
the one who never sleeps
never notices
too busy keeping the whole
flock of us
rolling towards vega
without losing
our milky way

goodnite big dad
hasta la vista
hasta luego
we'll switch on now
our own small stars
& lie in darkness burning
turning
through unspace untime
& upsadaisy back
i trust to you

South Laguna, California 1968

A SMALL FACULTY STAG FOR THE VISITING POET

but a large quantity of brandy
                on whisky
                on sherry

At one table's end the Necessary Dean
has broken out cigars
At the other the Oxonian Canon
splotchfaced now
is putting us all down with naughty quotes
from Persius we're too slow to get
—except the Czech professor & the Hungarian
who dig everything
so civilised they're savage with disappointment
in us all & no doubt saying so this moment
safely across my chest in at least 2 languages

somewhere in the smoke the Librarian
is heard toasting the cummunwealth
& feck the Yenks
The Padre winces & gradually
like Yahweh in the Zohar withdraws his presence
leaving behind that vacuum of Evil
which is us

The Physics Department's chief cultural exhibit
also a very anthropologetical Native Son
have just asked me unanswerable questions
simultaneously from across the centrepiece

I am the dead eye of this verbal typhoon
I am the fraudulent word-doctor
stripped to dumbness by their tribal ritual
I am neither civilised nor savage but also Necessary

                grinning
                & stoned
                & desolate

Australia 1968

MUSEUM OF MAN

the trustful curator has left me alone
in the closed wing of the aboriginal section

what's here?
3000 spears from arnhemland
waiting for a computer
to calculate their principle of balance

but what's in those wooden drawers?
i peek—sheeeez! shrunken heads
from new guinea
& dozens upon dozens
of twelve-inch penis sheaths

i'm going to lock doors
plant spears at windows
& try on everything for size

Adelaide 1968

CHRISTCHURCH, NZ

I have just flown 1100 miles from Australia
& landed in a Victorian bedroom
They sent up cindered muttonchops for lunch
There is an elderly reporter in my room with pince-nez
He wants to know why I have sideburns
& if I dont think being patronized by the Canada Council
isnt dangerous for my art or dont I feel I need to suffer?
In stone outside my window Capt. Scott
is nobly freezing to death near the South Pole
Suddenly I know the reporter is right
Sideburns have been sapping my strength

1968

FOUR FEET BETWEEN

I was extending a patchwork of lint & batten
from ankle-sores to my new heel-cuts
absorbed in masochism & blessing my foresight
with bandaids   blessing too the voyagers
who brought breadfruit to Fiji
& this tree casting a benison of leaves
just where the volcano trail widens down
to the islet's only road
(though i'd conceded to myself
there were some million years of hindsight
before the breadfruit learned to grow
3-foot leaves & cannonball-sized seeds
to come to terms with perpetuity)
The cotton foliage on my purpling feet
argued however that i'd learned nothing much
from 60 years of being literate
nothing about coral poison anyway
or the agility of lava to mince mainland shoes

I was cosseting a raw big toe with my last band
when i grew conscious a slow pad of other feet
was on the trail   so close when i looked up
i caught myself in the eyes deeplocked in a great face
Bula i said   trying to get it bass & guttural
His brows rose like wings   *Bula bula!* he said
quickly & stepped back
I must have got my hello close
& waited now for that wide Melanesian grin of welcome
But his stare was pitchy & the long bones of his face
seemed set in suspicion   even hostility
I could read nothing of him nor guess his age
the skin rough leather but the blast of hair
sootblack as any youth's
My height & about twice my width he stood there
a dark tree of flesh on the basalt stones

Suddenly he spoke   but in Fijian
i fumbled out my 7 words to say I couldnt speak it
He went back to staring   & i to my toepatch
Rooster-crows had been filtering thru the mangroves
There must be a village close   & he from it
I tried to forget it was near here only 90 years ago
these natives ate their last missionary
A bulbul began bulbulling in the breadfruit overhead
It stopped & there was only the far surf breathing
& the two of us

Mis-e-ter   yalo vinaka   He groped for English
police a wat you name a?   E-ro-la i said *what's yours?*
He muttered something cave-deep & gruff
no way i could repeat it   Should i try standing
& shaking hands?   But now his arms flew wide
and gestured at the road   *You wait a for bussy?*
Toot toot?   His eyes went back to my feet
I told him i'd just been swimming in the crater falls
was returning to the guesthouse in the port
He dug some of that perhaps   but threw out a big chest
made swimstrokes & waved at the lagoon   *Wy you tw?—*
Swim back by sea? i filled in   & tried
against a steady wrinkling of sepia forehead
to tell him i'd been snorkelling all week
just for the fun but got rolled on the coral
& the port doctor warned me off reefs
till the sores healed but then today i'd—
But he'd lost me near the start   Brows furrowed
like walnuts he bent over me   mouth muscles agonized
to find the right sounds   *Yeara   ow mucha yeara you?*
Sixty-five i said & fingered it   For the first time
he smiled   *Me!* he nodded his tall pompom
me too   *sickyfi'!*

That spark had leaped the wordgulf   We were egged on
I learned he'd even heard of Canada   *far side a Hawaii*
though he'd been born in the rooster's village
My lord i thought   he's only one generation
from Cannibal King Thakembau   I began pulling on my sox
& asked him if he'd been as far as Suva
His busby shook   *Sa sega   No alla tima here*
He looked more proud than sad
With a mahogany finger then he made an airy circle
You? You go rowna worela? Io i said *Yes*
& felt ashamed   He turned as if satisfied
but swung back & flung out at last the real question
E-ro-la   wat wrong a you feet?

I tried again & got nowhere   This wasnt tourist country
He'd never met a fullgrown man who went up the volcano
without a boar-spear   & swam in cold waterfalls
& dived in the sea only to be looking
But most of all he couldnt understand what hurt my feet
And so he stood   a statue of Melanic Power
maroon cheeks under a storm of hair
torso cicatriced with the darker scars of tribal rites
endured a half-century ago   a skirt of sorrel reeds
& all mounted on two unfeeling pedestals of meat
two tough sun-barbecued planksteaks of feet
like those his cousins use   across the bay on Benga
to walk on white-hot stones   for magic or for tourists

What's wrong my feet i said *is I not born here too*
He laughed   the only time   with a solid flash of teeth
Bussy come a some a time he said gently *you be o rite*
Ni sa mothe Goobye   He went paddling swiftly up the trail
You o-rite now i called   & lay back to wait the bus
under the breadfruit tree

Levuka 1969

ON THE NIGHT JET

small waffle-irons glowing
on a huge farmhouse stove
crossroad towns of the prairies
seven miles below

faint rods of highways
electroscopic genes

mainly only the stars
of the farms
lonely as the others
like reflections above
(below?)
and as remote
from me
now
on the night
jet

Over Saskatchewan 1970

WINDOW SEAT

40 ft of wing out there
suddenly i want to walk
into that sun
but capt loudspeaker says
headwinds 105 mph speed another 400
at once im walking back on air

!BUT WHAT A FUN DEATH!

                              alt 35000
                           nothing but
                 7
          miles of
high dive
at last i can practice   k
    g   c   n
  a   a   i
      i   j   f
                                  e
  r s   n   s
     e

                      o   a   r
                  b   d
s   p   r   i   n   g   i
                              n
                              g

down
     from   c l o u d
                      to   c l o u
                                     d
(o yes acceleration 32 ft per sec per sec)
but ive 7 m to play with
& all that wind d r i f t
    b
&   o d y f l a p

ive got time at last to break the world
's record for b (i once dreamed about) s ^{o} m
       a   e
       c   r
       k   s
                     ^{a}u ^{l}t

before straightening into a   s
         A A
         S S
        W W
          A A
    N N N N N N N N
          Ɐ

so widearmed & precise i am

embracing   s^e^{e}
             $_e$ $_e$!

the whole world & time
in one last sweet tick of li—

but no one lets me walk out
too hard to break this doubleglass
i'll have to be content again
with the usual smooth landing
dead on
& the meek shuffle into the pens
to wait my turn somewhere
at ground level
under the overcast ahead.

Edmonton, Alberta 1969

FROM THE BRIDGE: FIRTH OF FORTH

blood veins
of the flowering gorse
run down
to the blind waters

terns
dive on the islets
and salt the ruins
of castles
built in the second world war

under the butterflies
of yachts
how long the shadow
of the nuclear submarine

En route to Aberdeen 1971

CANADA: CASE HISTORY: 1973

No more the highschool land
deadset in loutishness
This cat's turned cool
the gangling's gone
guffaws are for the peasants

Inside his plastic igloo now
he watches gooks and yankees bleed
in colour on the telly
But under a faded Carnaby shirt
ulcers knife the rounding belly

Hung up on rye and nicotine and sex-
y flicks, kept off the snow and grass
he teeters tiptoe on his arctic roof
(ten brittle legs, no two together)
baring his royal canadian ass
white and helpless in the global winds

Schizoid from birth, and still a sado-masochist
this turkey thinks that for his sins
he should be carved while still alive:
legs to Quebec, the future Vietnam;
the rest, self-served and pre-digested,
to make a Harvest Home for Uncle Sam....

Teeth shot and memory going
(except for childhood grudges),
one moment murderous, the next depressed,
this youth, we fear, has moved from adolescence
into what looks like permanent senescence.

Toronto

NO BODY
(coming home from the airport)

i walk home in snow-slush
plodding alone imagining
the leap of pulse
under your greywool glove

snow slants down
an endless flock
of tiny bird-flakes
over me they wheel
and for a while move upward
having nowhere to fall
since you went away

the flat's not real
like a room "restored"
in a Pioneer Museum
exact but unconvincing
where is the being
who gave the armchair meaning?
i do not think
the tv will turn on

your small slippers
wait by the chesterfield
they do not move
something arranged
by a slick director
they lack the feet
which are human and complete
with minuscule calluses

i water the yellow chrysanthemum
silent as a photograph
nothing drinks
the armchair
stiff with air

only the bed grows
and is heard
it is twice as big already
and noisily empty
and yet an imitation too
a stuffed animal
nothing warm under the fur
no
body

Alexander Street, Toronto 1973

BIRTHDAY

Some nine hundred fifty circlings of my moon
i doubt i'll see a thousand
my face lunar now too
strings of my limbs unravelled
trunk weak at the core   like an elm's

worse   the brain's chemistry out of kilter
memory a frayed net
speech a slowing disc the needle jumps

& yet i limp about   insist in fact
on thanking the sky's pale dolphin
for flushing & plumping herself once more
into a pumpkin—
that storybook Moon still in my child mind
too deep for any astronaut to dig out

& stubbornly i praise the Enormous Twist
that set my sun to spinning me
these 26,663 times on the only known planet
that could sprout me

i praise too the great god Luck
that grew me into health
(out of mumps, chicken pox, measles, pneumonia, scarlet
fever, enteritis & a dozen broken bones)
Luck that freed me to roam & write
that gave me a lifetime of friends

some dawns it's true came up with betrayal
failure   rejection   bombs dropping
they taught me only happiness had been
& could be again

Sophocles said it's better not to be born
but he waited till 90 to tell us
at 74 i'm too young to know

so i bless whatever stars
gave me a cheerful father
with a bold heart & a dancing body
who passed me his quick eye & ear
& his faithful love-affair with words

& how can i not be grateful
to a Universe that made
my most enduring mother?
she too valued Luck   but she bet on Pluck
If ever deed of mine achieved
a glint of the unselfish
it was a fallen spark
from her lifetime's fire

when i give my dust to the wind
it will be with thanks
for those fellow earthlings
who forgave or forgot
my onetime wife   our son   our grandsons
& those comrades who held me
steady on cliffs

above all
my gratitude to whatever Is above all
to the young who light my evening sky
& to her   my happiest Happenstance—
if she remember me with love
when she is old
it will be immortality enough

FAMILY PICNIC IN GRAN CANARIA

No rain for seven years
There'll be no rain
on this offshore island of the Sahara
Only dews and sea-mists
bless these horny flowers
where father grips his ancient camera

In the finder is his little daughter
a Spanish curl to the lips
soft as the agave's petals
Cuddled between mama and grandpa
she strains to be still

Under the shining skull
he has bared
the old man is thinking
        this is my granddaughter
        there will be this record
        see already the hips are a woman's

Sidelong the mother watches
a dog curving to the lunch basket
She is told to smile

High and white the sun rides
over the volcano
squeezing their eyes to raisins
Even the child's face wrinkles
in the savage light

The prophetic camera
engraves against the lava slope
the suffering cheeks
the anxious foreheads
Grandfather overexposed
will be death-white
There will be despair in all mouths
hard-ridden by the sun.

Agaete, June 1976

HALFPERSON'S DAY

halfawake on my side of the bed
my arm moves to emptiness
fumbles on Mr. Toad our Totem
lying stuffed & lugubrious
between me & the vacancy

there's only one peach to be peeled
one bowl one spoon one mouth
my red vitamin lacks a golden mate
one porch chair in the rising sun
the Globe turns in silence

to write is good perhaps
but her dark eyes flower above my page
i sound my scribbles in a solitude
the inner ear is only
halflistening

the telephone
"no... she'll be back in 13 days"
(plus 4 hours & 13 nights)

alone in the apartmenthouse pool
32 lengths   who cares?
back at the flat door i push my key
into our lock
withdraw to emptiness

wander to the piano
at least there's no one
to hear my mistakes
—but Mozart without her
is just a sit-up

so i do real sit-ups
or halfdo them
no one holding firm
to my good ankle

i take the partial body out
though walking's not a walk
a walk takes two takes me takes her

lie down at last in blackness
Toad's on the blanket still
too still   a limp perversion
beside a demiperson
plunging a schizophrenic head
into her pillow's almond bodysmell
i drown in something
yesterday we called our bed

Balliol Street 1977

DECREE ABSOLUTE (FOR ESTHER)

we remember strangely the first hurts from love
the young are pierced through by their passions

you must not grow ancient   poor dear
but quickly old enough to forget
this last aggression

it will be enough to carry
to our separate deaths
the memory of the first time
i stung you to tears

twenty-five and loving and we at last together
while beyond the window of our train
all Kent was singing with appleblossoms
shaken by the bees

Canterbury 1935–Toronto 1975

THREE FOR ALISON

1. i think you are a whole city

& yesterday when i first
touched
you i started moving
thru one of your suburbs
where all the gardens are fresh
with faces of you
flowering up

some girls are only houses
maybe a strip
development
woman you are
miles of boulevards   with supple
trees unpruned & full of winding
honesties

so give me   give me
time   i want   i want
to know all your squares &
cloverleafs   ime steering now
by a constellation winking over
this night's rim from some great
beachside of you with highrisers & a spotlit
beaux arts

i can hear your beating centre will i
will i make it   are there maps of
you i keep circling   imagining parks
fountains arcades all your stores

back in my single bed
i wander
your stranger   dreaming
i am your citizen

The Beaches, Toronto 1965

2. there are delicacies

there are delicacies in you
     like the hearts of watches
there are wheels that turn
     on the tips of rubies
& tiny intricate locks

i need your help
     to contrive keys
there is so little time
     even for the finest
          watches

Scarborough 1966

3. *i should have begun with your toes*

with maybe just the little one
so clean & succulent
so tiny
it's no toe at all
but a spare nipple   ummmm

now the big one
big? the nail on it so weeny
& silvery
it's more like a stamp-hinge
to hold down some rarity
a pink imperforate
engraved in *taille douce*

& you've got ten
all in mint condition

& now let's forget
philately
& up the golden stairs!

Waterloo, September 1967

STILL LIFE NEAR BANGALORE

The painter quiets all but his busy brush.
The writer is obsessed to ask: what next?

> My train creeps blindly through this canvas
> towards old Bangalore. Nearest my window,
> right, an oxcart moves (or stops?)
> on a pinched black road where jacarandas
> leave magenta bruises, and a pair of women
> stand face to shadowed face beneath tiered baskets.
> They are compositions of sky-blue shawls
> and sable braids aslant down chalky saris.
> Merchant's wives, I'd guess, with time to gossip.
> Left, their road elbows, vanishes with palms.

Beyond the oxcart the emerald paddyfields
submit to yoked brute buffalo.
Indifferent geometrists they draw in ochre mud
their sinuous counter-patterns.
Behind each slatey team an almost naked
human beast, bareheaded, breached with rags,
is ploughing (with a stick, is it?, clutched
in raddled hands) while a companion guides
their Shivas by a rope. It threads the sacred
nostrils. They steer around the corpse-like
sleeping cows and boulders huge as bones
of long-drowned mastodons.

The background, between bamboo strokes
and breadfruit blobs, is giving hints
of lizard-tawny thatch (the village
of those still, still-talking matrons?)
Near a splash of wall where a *flamboya* burns
dim figures walk with trays, perhaps of frangipani
for an unseen temple. Or of sandalwood?
(My window cannot smell.)

But what kind of cloud on that horizon
is swelling silently from jungle into sky?
And what will happen here beside me
as round the bend to Bangalore
comes sudden mounting filling the road
a ten-ton oil truck? It is surely
roaring, blaring, screeching out its warnings?
(My window cannot hear.)

In that second when they slid forever from my ken
did those women leap away? that cloud subside?
Or towered to fill their sky with fire so bright
no painter's brush no writer's thought
will ever stay to catch it?

India 1972

CRY OVER ASWAN

a sound has roused me   a gull screeching?
no   it's night still   i slip from our hostel bed
to the balcony   the Big Dog is leashed
to the bright nail of Sirius in silence
almost absolute   i hear only a dying cough
from the lone watchman below in the camel-yard
and in a smudge of palms the Saharan winds
scratching like crabs   i turn back to bed

but suddenly again that cry
a woman's voice   not near   not far   urgent
from the maze of workmen's tents by the dam?
peril or nightmare? a passion sped that scream!
i think fear...but of what?   rape?   murder?

i have no phone   no Arabic   only male guilt
beyond my railing now the dawn blurs
over Elephant Island, those rocks the Nile gnawed
to a funeral boat immense enough to ferry
fifty centuries of Nefertitis off to Nowhere
brief bark of a dog   Canubis   half-wild now
by the edges of tombs, the guide said
guarding still   or howling a mate?
the human call is not repeated

behind i hear my dearest waking murmurous
from a dream of bawdry (with me, she says)
her artless laughter sets me on fire
as naked in the sheets we launch once more
with wanton cries the fragile vessel
of our own brief day

Egypt 1974

FALL BY FURY

Now was the season
summer so high and still
the birds in the circling woods
held all the tale

Past deserted nests I rose
through a world of web with swede-saw
severing
dropping
the black treebones
for the consummation of winter fire
O through the brace and embrace
of a hundred living arms I swung
gathering delight in my own ease
muscle and breath at a play of skill

I was climbing the tall beech
to prune dead limbs
that overhung the summer home
before some gale might hurl
a snag into glass

Each grasp tugged at the old zest
for a climb:
the rock-fort a year back
in Sri Lanka
and before in my sixties
up the yellow spines of Australia's Olgas...
at fifty-eight in the cloudy Andes on the ribs
of Huayna Picchu at thirty
inching down English chalk on Lulworth cliffs
... twenty-one and over the icy necks
of the Garibaldis and before that
the cliffs of my teens ... Temple...
Edith... all the climbings
made in joy of the sport
and never with hurt to me or to others

as now to the topmost vault
of the beechtree's leaves I rose
to the flooding memories
of childhood
perched in my first treehouse
safe in its green womb

Where brittle branches had threatened
a tunnel of light
shone up to me now
as i sat in the secrets of leaf
and smiled on the innocent roof
that hid my love preparing our noon-day meal

Shining ahead was the fortnight
given us here alone by our friends
to swim with the small fish in their pond
read and doze in the sun
hide in the sumac to watch
the little fox by their den
or to work with hands on wood
and heart on words
rhythms already shaping themselves
in the piney air
this first of the mornings

So I threw the last snag down
and the locked saw after
turning and shifting my grips
to descend to Wailan
when something   my Hubris
some Fury of insect wind and sting
drove its whining hate at my eye
One hand unloosed
convulsive to shield
and I slipped
forever from treetops

Caught in a yielding chair of air
I grasped and grasped
at a speeding reel

of branches half-seized
and wrenched away
by the mastering will
of the earth
The next bough surely—
my hard mother
crushed me limp in her stone embrace
stretched me still
with the other limbs
laid my cloven hip and thigh
with those I had cleft

And that was a world
and two summers ago
yet still in the night I reach
for holds eluding my clutch
till the moment comes
when the Furies
relent

I catch and cling
swoop
alight on friendly ground

and run again on two good feet
over the grass of dream

Toronto 1977

ELLESMERELAND III

At last in Ellesmereland's hotels
for a hundred fifty each per night
we tourists shit down plastic wells
and watch tv by satellite
The "land beyond the human eye"
the Inuit call it still...
Under the blinding midnight sky
subs and missiles wait our will

1985

CANADA: CASE HISTORY: 1985

[File Update] This is now no high-school land
Adult & schizoid he admits to thinking sometimes
he is the Third World's Saviour.
But then his mood will swing
from euphoria to complainings
(oil is leaking from his arctic roof)
Depression triggers nightmares:
he is a tightrope clown
but with ten brittle legs no two in step.
"Or," he says shyly, "I'm in my Mountie uniform
but my pants have slipped.
I'm standing bare-assed in the arctic winds."
Given Rorschach he found a turkey
...decapodal...which he would carve alive.
"Drumsticks," says he, "I'd promise to the West.
Wings to the Atlantic; Ontario the neck,
giblets for the tundra, breast to Quebec.
But first I'd pass the platters down to Uncle.
He has the cutlery. And anyway
it's his Thanksgiving Day
we really keep."

FOR WAILAN

BEGINNING

the miracle leaps
in the sap unseen
under the scarred elm's bark
to a skyfull of buds

the truth runs
from the old
hands on the keys
to the song in the young throat

the magic flows
in the wind that bends
the waterlily's face
to the lips of the wrinkling lake

Uxbridge 1973/1985

SHE IS

(for Wailan, on her twenty-fourth birthday)

she is
a little spruce tree
fresh every way
herself
like a dawn

when warm winds come
she will move
all her body
in a tremble of light

but today she stands
in magical stillness
she has clasped
all my falling flakes
from the round of her sky
and wished them
into her own
snowtree

through the cold time
she holds me
with evergreen
devotion
she bears up my whiteness

o so light may i press
letting each needle
grow in her own
symmetry
for i am at peace
in her form
after whirling
and faithful to all
her curves

but when warm winds come
we must stir from this trance
she will lift living arms
to the sun's dance

i will slide then
in a soft caress
of her brown sides
and my falling will end
somewhere in her roots

may my waters then
bring her strength only
help her hold trim
and evergreen her being
with suns and winds
for o many and many
and happiest years

Treehouse, Uxbridge 1974

FATHER GROUSE

some mornings trying to write
i get like an old ruffed partridge
flopping off & on the nest
scared somebody'll steal
those handsome brown eggs
i've never quite laid yet

flinching from cloud shadows
hearing a fox behind every bush
snakes in the grass
shots on the hill—
limping & trembling around
from what looked like a man
but was only a dumb moose—
till i crumble down beat
with nothing done
& then the phone rings

but listen!
it isn't another mag salesman
or the Poets' League about dues
out of that lovely earpiece
comes a voice spreading sunshine
all through the woods
& i sit back drumming softly
to the loveliest partridge of all
(whose eggs they really are)
& feeling energy-control
right down to my wingtips

after we hang up
quietly i'm warming the eggs again
if i can't lay i can hatch
maybe something of me
will show in the chicks

Alexander Street 1974

BESTIARY

an arkfull she is
of undulant creatures
a cinnamon bearcub
curled in a warm ball
thinking of honey & berries
nuts roots or even
grass jelly for supper

a sturdy raccoon too
with masked eyes
& dexterous forepaws
very frequent to bathe
& a bandit of ice cream
who sleeps a lot
with one soft hindpaw
poking most modestly out

or a shy bobcat
coloured olive-brown
or maybe pale gold
with round
slipper-fur feet
on which she sits very quiet
and so thoughtful
beside her leafy plants
she is sometimes invisible
though very much there

she can be an ochre
squirrel as well
sinuous & all compact
alert & frisky
& away & back like a dream
& whatever creature
she is its peaceful emissary
most faithful
& most loving

Toronto 1974

OMNIBUS

a new city bus she is too
neat & with her own
not always predictable
route to travel

it's a pleasure just to wait
peer up the street
& here she comes
nimble & quick
but caring for kids
& polite to trucks

with small sneezes she stops
& glides me away
the only passenger
while the people outside
fall silent & take on colour
she has put them on tv
with the sound off
now nothing needs to be understood
& anyone might be a hero

behind the clear round
of her windows
through a still possible world
she carries me loving
& safe in herself

Davisville Avenue 1975

DREAM BEYOND DEATH

from the dark pit
hand firm in hand
we walk up a sunfilled slope
the strange flowers above
bless us and beckon
escaped from time past
we are seven now both
i too am chinese
our obsidian eyes are bright
the fresh-peeled nectarines
in our cheeks

there is no need to talk
we know we are mounting at last
to our rightful life
waiting over the rim
we hear already the birds in song
we bring from our first world
only the one heart's pacer
we fashioned together

its pulse is lifting us now
to twice ten thousand days
we will have time at last
to become and beget
before fading
still loving
as one

i wake
and return to this vision
feeling our linked hands
more certain than all existence
this dream from desire is lava-deep
i cannot believe death's cold crater
will contain it

Scarborough Hospital, July 1975

ON HER TWENTY-SIXTH

At six you folded paper boats
with nowhere to sail them down
except a tub in Chinatown

Sixteen you climbed into a dory
to heave through sloughs of English Lit
and came by a dying lake to sit

Then we shaped our own canoe
birch-delicate but strong
and big enough for two

Over the portage freed
we steer through rapids worth the battling
They flow to a living sea

Sit straight dear twenty-six
hold firm the blade you've made
Mine dips with yours however frayed

With luck and will we'll reach
at last some bronzed arbutus beach
From there you'll sail the world

Give my old paddle then a simple burning
Sift the ashes down
where the fish and weed are turning

But today   sweet twenty-six
rest your eyes from the current's shine
loose your small palms from the coursing
let them find mine.

January 1976

172

ZOOS HAVE BARS

Your voice abstracts in a telephone
from melody to monotone
while me the instrument allows
only grunts and male meows
I need your eyes to shine my love on
This doesnt have your melon smell on
I want to squeeze real flesh and bone
unloosed from the clutch of a telephone.

Balliol Street 1976

FUSION

no welding
of ores or floes
no liquation
of salt pillars
no sunthaw of drift
deliquescence of hardness
is like the melding
wherever my bones
fuse & dissolve
in your soft body
& we sleep into one
twinned
& twined
till we wake

and rise
still
welded

Toronto, March 1976

NEVER BLUSH TO DREAM
(to a melody in the "Chrysanthemum Rag" of Scott Joplin)

1

never blush to dream
a lost love
slides into your bed again

there's no treason
though the blood stirs
when a stranger speaks his name

> each lover keeps the home
> he made within your mind
> and has a key
> to lie with you unbidden
> so long as you are holding
> gentle thoughts of him

2

never feel a guilt
to hear me
whisper still within the night

old loves lurk in eyes
that brighten
to the new enchanter's sight

i too must rise from warmth
to drift with other ghosts
from worldly view
yet i'll come into your bed
some night again
and dream myself alive in you

Toronto 1977

174

FALL IN SPRING

i'm going to be real mad
if it dies
    wailan sprays briskly
    the potted rosebush
    she womanhandled back to our flat
    a crimson cloud for easter

we wont let it
    i say firmly
    but puzzled what alchemy
    the local plantshop used
    to trick this rambler
    into april resurrection

    wailan does not wonder
    being twenty-seven she believes
    i can keep the sap alive
    even at seventy-two

    after three days
    the blossoms wreathe our floor

April 1977

COMING BACK FROM THE AIRPORT

the flat's not real
a room restored
in a period museum
exact but unconvincing
i do not believe the tv
will turn on

your small slippers
poke from under the chesterfield
something arranged
by a slick director
they do not move
lacking the brown feet
which were human
with minute calluses

i water the chrysanthemum
silent as a photograph
nothing drinks
the armchair
stiff with air

only the bed
grows & is heard
twice as big
petrified with tousling
& yet an imitation too
a stuffed animal

nothing warm under the fur
no
body

July 1977

MOMENT OF ECLIPSE (1)

4 p.m.
moon's umbrage slides over Sun
we are a lozenge in His mouth
the owl has hushed
light dries
chills
only the other suns flare out
strange shadows are rippling
over the birch trunks
and sudden fireflies around the porch
are coldly dancing

i see my love 5000 kilometres away
walking in the noonday Sun
wordless i feel her lips
move into mine

September 1977

MOMENT OF ECLIPSE (2)

four on a summer's afternoon
suddenly the moon
slides over our Sun
and we are a lozenge in her mouth

that owl has hushed
light dries   chills
only the other suns
far away flare up...

on the birch trunks
without source
a riffle of shadows

around our porch
instant fireflies
coldly dancing

i glimpse
my love walking
three thousand miles away
in the noonday Sun

soundless the lips of another
move into hers

1977

DIVING

loving you i hold my breath
i dive from dryness
slide to softer meadows
where all is upsidedownness
silence   yielding
to silence

and then since love
is winged by words
wants air for launching
we heave aloft
are warmed in a glitter of sounds
flaked away by the wind

but loving you is beyond wings
is to dive and dive and
sway with primal weed
is to dance with fins
in a joy too salt
for sounding

1978

LOOKING UP
(for Wailan on her twenty-ninth)

love   you draw back
from the sight of maybe 70 more storeys
in the mist above

to stay on this level always
who wouldn't?   house plants everlasting
but the tenancy rule is one UP each year
or OUT

when i had to move to the 29th
i was so desperate i tried to block
the elevator with rejected manifestos

crazy?   we all know almost
nothing in this highrise goes DOWN
not even the stairs
& the management refuses escalators

    ime on the 74th & set to move
UP UP till ime really breathless
& the Super shoves me OUT the chute
with the garbage

but you & i   love
we dont let this bother us
we have our secret fire-escape
to go & come between floors
it lets me sit today beside your lilies
pecking out my certainty

the apartments further UP
will be even better for you
with whatever flatmate

love   let the Landlord worry
about next year's lease

sit with me now & look beyond the geraniums
at this moment's simple sky
in the best of all 29th storeys

Balliol Street, January 1979

WITH A RECORDER FOR LAN

a tree-stem
hollowed
8 holes   hidden in 1
is a fipple   a knob
edged to blow breath over
a blockflute

at stonehenge they found one
carved from a ram's bone
(and before that how many centuries
of herd-girls piping?)

held simply in the hands   end-blown
more basic than the wheel
and less pervertible

january 27, 1980
this one in a cardboard box
totally unpretending   like you
holding within
mysteries intangible
melodies climbing by magic intervals
from pastures to cathedrals

i hear your first notes
this birthday morning
one by plaintive one
they have already your gentleness
they strive for precision
yearn for the overtones   persist
toward song

love may the next thirty years
bring you time and recorders
to blow out in bravura
whatever is blocked unshared
misprized within you
and let there always be one
when i am deaf
who hears the music your breath makes
now in me   by merely breathing

Toronto, January 1980

OLD MAN BELIEVING IN SUMMER

believe this whisper
(even a husk may shape a prophecy)
believe i hear
among the young intrepid bees
that buzz your summer
one that will burst through pollen
singing
there will be berries brightening
before the autumn's burnish
while deep in wintered earth
i meld into your taproot
into the holdfast we made
in our spring

1981

JOYFUL DAY

to be alive with you is life enough
for singing any time
to wake beside you on your birthday
is to dance my january back to may

we watch beyond our window the ice-bright maples
cold-shouldering every snowflake
each unique geometry going down
to dissolution in the shapeless drifts

we see   but twined we stay
in love's warm garden on this happy day
this orchard where the flowering peach
fulfills a slip bequeathed from Chang-an's arbors
where poets walked   supped wine   made love
and music through perhaps as many centuries
as years you have today, sweet thirty-two

what? you sigh   some pink petals dropped already?
but that's lucky!   only the fallen float to poems
Li Po stared between such ambiguities to find
his love for Wong Lun all the deeper
(as mine, Wai Lan, for you)
This mottled leaf the winds of autumn overlooked
rides still to you

So be up, dear one, and see the clouds roll back
the sun contrive a glory from the spectral city
where we dumbly join the seven deadly dancers
but not this joyful Day

today we dance to our own tunings
safe in the garden of our Now
that we have grown   and by our embracing
still embraces us

1982

MY LOVE IS YOUNG

my love is young & i am old
she'll need a new man soon
but still we wake to clip and talk
to laugh as one
to eat and walk
beneath our thirteen-year-old moon

good moon   good sun
that we do love
i pray the world believe me
& never tell me when it's time
that i'm to die
or she's to leave me

Toronto 1973–1986

AVE ATQUE VALE

Over the hill and
sinking fast in the bog
i've time just to wave

one muddy hand

1986

WHEN WE MUST PART

sweetheart, think that my death
swings wide your harbour's mouth
to welcome in the young and joyful
the quick eyes ready for the searoads
time is yours for choosing
the love to sail the world with

(and the father to make with you
the unborn waiting to be loved)

if clouds hang heavy now
remember how your gentle sun
wheeled my rough planet round you
believe in my belief
that you were made to shine
with love
and being loved

swim proud dear princess
let no one dim
the brilliance of your mind
let no one bind
the courage of your heart

my small one so tall in patience
i think you will grow wise as Orcas
yet never lose your dolphin curves

1977/1986

E N D

Wailan dearest
in your spring
you took my arm
to walk with me
into my snowscape

You must tramp back now
Summer still waits for you
Make it be long
Let the sun fill it

Then autumn
with pumpkin and mangoes
a fireplace shared
to warm another
with the same love
you shone steadfast on me

If sometime my shadow
flits over the embers
it's just to bless.

1987

Earle Birney on Poetry

The Finding of Form

The writing of a poem is the search for its precise form, a series of decisions about "shape."

First, with "David," was it to be drama or non-drama? An easy answer: my subject was visually too grandiose, and humanly too restricted, to be natural on a stage. Non-dramatic, then.

Second, poetry or prose? More difficult to decide. The difference is not simply a visual matter of choosing between a solid right margin and paragraph breaks versus an irregular right margin and line breaks— even if many readers seem willing to believe anything broken up is verse and anything solid "only" prose. No, if I have my writing set in verse lines, I'm signalling to my readers that I'm about to use any of a number of techniques he doesn't normally expect to find in English prose and that indeed many prose writers consciously avoid.

Before I go further, I want to set down what I consider to be these special techniques to be expected in most poetry:

1. *Sound effects* intended, in part, to make the poem carry pleasures not only to the inner ear, but to others hearing it spoken or even chanted or sung. Traditional among such effects are:

    (a) *strong rhythms* or pulsations, repeated regularly or irregularly and indicated by line breaks, with sometimes the aid of spaces within lines and of punctuation.

       It's no go the merrygoround, it's no go the rickshaw,

    (b) *musical cadences* by means of rhymes, vowel or consonant chimings (assonance, consonance, alliteration) or equivalent discords, through a false-rhyme and dissonance.

       All we want is a limousine and a ticket for the peepshow.
                                    (Louis MacNeice, "Bagpipe Music")

2. *Repetitions* of key words, often with meaning shifts, and of dominant images and ideas, for purposes not only of emphasis (as in rhetorical prose) but of producing effects in the nature of

"spells" and "exorcisms"; a form of transference of what is haunting the poet into writing, to a haunting of those who read:

> The boot in the face, the brute
> Brute heart of a brute like you.
>> (Sylvia Plath, "Daddy")

3. *Concentrated expression*: the fewest possible words/sounds to say the most intended. No syllable without a function.

> Parting is all we know of heaven,
> And all we need of hell.
>> (Emily Dickinson, "#1732")

4. *Total verbal freedom* to use whatever kind of grammar and whatever level of word the poet feels will best convey his own true voice and the exact shades of meaning he intends. Syntax, the conventions of word order, all the solemn rules of college texts on "good English" are followed or ignored in the interest of effectiveness. "The best words in the best order." A drawing upon the total vocabulary of the English language, what our Anglo-Saxon ancestors called the "word-hoard." Words are the poet's medium, to be expended as the painter uses paint. By words alone the poet must create his colour, music, emotion, thought, his personal universe. In the interests of precision he may use technical terms, in the interests of atmosphere, archaic or exotic ones; he may need four-letter words or fourteeners, puns and other ambiguities, understatements to make over-feelings, words particularly charged by their original meanings, sudden leaps in thought, paradoxes, contradictions and fantastic challenges to the reader's imagination.

> I caught this morning morning's minion, kingdom of
> daylight's dauphin, dapple-dawn-drawn Falcon, . . .
>> (G.M. Hopkins, "The Windhover")

> anyone lived in a pretty how town . . .
> he sang his didn't he danced his did.
>> (e.e. cummings, "anyone lived . . .")

5. Despite all these sophistications, the surface clarity of a mountain stream (permitting glimpses of swirling depths, however, and hints of strange shadows and movements below). *The art of appearing simple and offering complexity*, leading the reader down from the word to the image to the symbol, and from the poet and his disguises, his "characters," to the reader's most secret self.

    > The night has a love for throwing its shadows around a man
    > a bridge, a horse, the gun, a grave.
    > (Charles Olson, "The K")

6. An assumption that readers and listeners will be willing and able to project beyond the poet's immediate thought, to draw on all their own resources of intelligence, sensitivity and human intuition, to explore their own subconscious, to match or excel the poet's—in short, to write their own poems while reading and listening to his. Dylan Thomas talked about "a main column of meaning" in his poems. It's the river image again. It's there in all but the dadaistic anti-poems; it carries the reader along with the poem, but is full of rapids and back currents. Every reader has to find his own way down to the sea. The poet writes out of *a faith in the existence of at least one reader*, someone who can share his vision and, yes, his love of humanity. Though we now seem to be creatures destined to destroy ourselves within a generation, we humans have within us still the power to rescue ourselves and all life. Poets are generally among the sharpest critics of existing civilization and societies but when a poet comes to believe that man is totally evil and without hope, he won't seek any longer for a reader. However, he'll continue to write.

    > And I am dumb to tell the lover's tomb
    > How at my sheet goes the same crooked worm.
    > (Dylan Thomas, "The force that through
    > the green fuse . . .")

7. This is because, for all his care to involve his audience, *a poet is in the first place writing for himself*. The act is a kind of confrontation and self-exploration done partly in an agony of search, partly in euphoric excitement, out of the fiercest honesty.

Verbal Patterns and Rhythms in "David"

The decisions about these had to come naturally from the ones already made about overall form, subject, setting, action, characters.

Obviously I needed a flexible metre to span the two widely separated moods of the poem that moved from carefree high spirits to numb disaster. A rhythm of ups and downs, then, but not bumping or dragging, always moving ahead.

It was at this point I began consciously to profit from the examples of some narrative poets whose techniques I'd admired. There was Stephen Vincent Benét and his *John Brown's Body*. But the great metrical variety maintained in that poem, through constantly changing stanzaic patterns, could happen only within the length of a book. Mine was to have the nature of a short short story, needing to keep to whatever was its basic rhythm in order not to blur the "single effect." The verse tragedies of Robinson Jeffers, on the other hand, so grandly mournful, were too much in monotone for my taste. The *Conquistador* of Archibald MacLeish, though also a much longer poem, was nearer to what I wanted. His mingling of anapests and iambs and amphibrachs produced effects of strength and zest as well as cadences of helplessness and sorrow: that combination could stagger, even crawl, or it could move, as Coleridge said, "with a leap and a bound." MacLeish had controlled his rhythm with assonance or vowel-rhyme, a device with which I had become familiar when I studied Old French in the graduate school of the University of California and read the eleventh-century *Chanson de Roland* in the original. I now reread it, and it helped me to weave my own sound-form, a dividend from my Berkeley days.

As soon as I began shaping lines, I had to make a decision about stanzas. The reader's eye becomes oppressed by pages of solid type (how many pages I didn't know). And yet I wanted a sense of continuous flow. I decided then to have stanza eye-breaks, but to keep both rhythm and sense flowing, with only the most natural breath-breaks, forward from line to line and line-group to line-group—what the French call *enjambement*.

This process did produce an adventurous pace, but it was a little too fast. It would not create in the voice of Bob that sense of recall, that feeling of the adult looking back, sobered by a tragedy still obsessive in his memory, which my structure required. The poem must be his counterspell against the madness of remembering. I thought of Chaucer, remembering perhaps the passions and agonies of his own youth in *Troilus and Criseyde*, and of Coleridge's "Rime of the Ancient Mariner," in which echoing rhyme produces these effects. But I was afraid that too much rhyme would slow the story, even distract from it. And yet no rhyme at all, such as in blank verse, might be too wooden. I decided to make an assonantal pattern of *abba* for my stanzas and hold to it throughout. I think if "David" does create moods of nostalgia and fatality, celebrating youthful heroism and yet elegizing its loss, it's partly because of the sonorous cadences these technical devices produce. So the poem is in debt to earlier poets who showed us all how such things can be done.

*   *   *   *

Another formal aspect of the poem that developed during its writing was a structural use of images. Some of these, such as the skeleton of the goat, and the crippled robin, devices drawn from my own memories, are there to foreshadow the accident and the choice David will make when he finds himself as doomed as the robin. More extensively, I was careful to place a series of words and images in the first part that suggested vitality, youthfulness, joy, energy (an example is "lengthening coltish muscles") and to counterpose them later with symbols of horror and deadness. The long journey up the Finger is described as seen by the two climbers in a mood of sunshiny adventure and merry daring. At the end, the same details reappear in reverse order, suffused with lonely horror: first the peak (now "wind-devilled"), then the chimney, the shining seracs (now "fanged and blinding") and so on.

Beyond this more cerebral carpentry, however, images more satisfying to me welled up of themselves as the poem grew into shape. Without realizing it, I developed a sequence of metaphors (pointed out later by critics) drawn from oceans, the "alien prairie," and even from outer space, to set mountains and nature against the fleeting lives of men. Similarly, certain words became keys that repeated themselves without my knowledge (for example "splayed," lines 41 and 106). Some of these worked, others were less happy.

Even the storyline made a twist or two of its own, memory suddenly supplying useful details I hadn't known I knew: a phenomenon familiar to all writers in the heat of creating. Some psychologists have described it as the tapping of the unconscious, that mysterious central source of the brain's energy, an involuntary search-and-discovery of what may be the primordial images we've inherited from the dawn of prehumanity. It doesn't, of course, follow that "David" is a great poem, even if it could be shown to contain essential myths and archetypal images of the race. I'm saying only that however negligible my poem is when set against the memorable ones of our language, I did experience, in writing it, a rush of imagic energy and excitement beyond and above my rational control. Certain psychiatrists recognize this as a state experienced by many psychotic patients. As Norman Hirt mentions in *The Psychoanalysis of Creativity*, the act of writing takes on a "compelling visional sensitivity," welding conscious and unconscious existence together, and suspending any sense of time in a burning waking dream. It's a temporary state, fortunately for the poet's hold on legal sanity, but a peculiarly intense one for him, of all artists, since he's the one who relies most perhaps on this welling up of charged images to communicate his deepest emotions.

When that flow dwindles, a merely verbal one may continue, and deceive the poet into thinking he's still writing effectively. Writing is a form of intoxication. There's a euphoric "high"; then next morning the hangover. You look at what you've written and realize the last hour was spent saying it all wrong; the verbal compulsion kept going after the imagic rush slowed down. In my case, I suspect I begin to fail at the point where I lose *any* conscious control of the flow, and what might be poetry becomes automatic rhetoric and cliché. *Total* freedom from discipline is a merely negative state. So it often was with "David." And the scars of my nightly defeats are still visible to me in the poem. However, there came a time, some two months after I "saw" that mountain on Bloor Street, when the poem was finished.

But what did "finishing" mean? It meant simply that I gave up trying to make it better, to write it yet again (after at least three

190

complete rewritings). I ceased struggling to make what I had match the glowing dream I'd started with. I settled for something that was a measure of my own limitations, the point where I could no longer see holes in plot or characterization, or places needing lengthening or shortening, tightening or loosening, or anywhere demanding further heightening of the levels of meaning. The sounds and swayings of the words, when I read the poem again aloud to myself, seemed at last consistent, with the dissonances happening only when I wanted. However much further other poets might have gone, I'd stopped because I couldn't see beyond.

Now, thirty years later, the descriptions seem to me a little lush and self-conscious, the characters underdeveloped, the brief moments of dialogue a bit wooden, the symbolic under-substance shallow, even trite. But maybe these are simply an old man's inability to appreciate himself-when-young. In any case, I couldn't at that time see any way to remedy such defects, even if I could have admitted them, without frustrating my main purpose.

And that, as I could see now I'd "finished" it, was to tell a story about mountains in which the mountains became a character, a personality against whom two youths deliberately matched themselves. They were young men endowed with that intense sensitivity of youth and its capacity for physical joy. And the story was about how they came to the sudden loss of all those endowments through a sort of *hubris*, an overconfident pride in their ability to win all their challenges of the other character. It was truly the tale of "that day, the last of my youth on the last of our mountains"; though even that ending line was unplanned, came blessedly in the final moments of groping with the ultimate rewrite.

Yet what did it all add up to as a statement? Man cannot live in nature without subservience to nature? Wisdom destroys innocence? "In the midst of life we are in death"? Life can be lived to the full only by risking the loss of it? Or some other bromide? You can reduce all poetry to philosophic cliché, all mine at any rate, but I've long ceased to worry that "David" is vulnerable to this kind of intellectual heckling, and it doesn't seem to have troubled even its harshest critics.

The "Meaning" of a Poem

This is a phrase used by persons who assume a poem has only one meaning, and they ought to know it. The meaning of "David" is what I put into it plus anything else you get out of it. In my poem, the meaning is almost always more than what is apparently there, and operates on various levels. It also varies according to the reader's basic language abilities and sensitivities, his acquaintance with other literature and with the background of the poem.

In any case, clarity, as I have said before, is only on the surface of a serious poem, and you will be all the more drawn into it because of that. No great art is ever enjoyed fully at first acquaintance. The language of poetry is complex, ambiguous, cunning and highly personal. It's not the language of your daily newspaper. It doesn't yield up single "right" answers to examination questions any more than life does. Perhaps the best way to get full meaning out of a poem is to forget about meaning when you read it.

Instead, see with it, smell with it, touch with it, and above all hear with it. A poem is a total sensuous experience.

El Greco: *Espolio*

In 1953 I saw a retrospective El Greco exhibition in Bordeaux. One painting that both captured and puzzled me was his *Espolio*, an imagining of the scene when Christ waited on the Hill of Calvary before his execution. Meantime he endured the Espolio or "spoliation" (Latin *expolio*, that is, "despoiling"), a tearing away of his clothes by greedy spectators who would then gamble for the strips. In this painting, there is a prominent figure in the right foreground, in workmen's clothes, whom I take to be the carpenter; he is busy putting holes in the cross.

Seven years after I saw the original in Bordeaux, a publisher sent me a cropped reproduction of the *Espolio*, which focussed attention on the lower half of the painting, and so on the carpenter. I realized that someone else must surely have been caught by the strangeness of making the most immediate figure in the painting not Christ but his executioner. I now noticed also that the eyes of the Virgin and the other women were fixed on this same subsidiary figure, whose back was actually turned to Christ. What was El Greco driving at?

We'll never know for sure but we can all make guesses. I took the publisher's ad away with me that weekend to a friend's place on Bowen Island, my writing retreat in those years. And my own guess began to verbalize inside me. But the poem that resulted wasn't really a guess; I was far too unskilled as an interpreter of visual art to come forward with any "thesis" about El Greco's canvas. All I could try to do was to unravel the thoughts it had set going in my head, to think about craftsmanship, one of the elements in art that links its creator with carpenters, engineers, farmers, housewives, with everybody who employs a skill to earn a living. There's a curious peace that comes in the intensity of practising one's métier, an absorption that annihilates time and place.

If what I've just said isn't clear to the student, this is a good time for him to look up *Matthew* 27:35, or *Mark* 15:24, or *Luke* 23:34–35, or best of all, *John* 19:23–24, and become perhaps more confused. In El Greco's painting, the garments are being taken off, as one might expect, *before* the actual crucifying; in all four gospels, it seems they crucify him first.

From *The Cow Jumped over the Moon,* 1972

Why Poetry? (I)

So you do listen to poetry; you even listen to me talking about it. But why? Well, I can tell you what Confucius said, many centuries ago, in his *Analects.* That philosopher found half a dozen reasons for reading poetry, the first of which would be hard to guess. It helps us, he said, to remember the names of birds, animals, plants, trees. The poem is a mnemonic primer!—a function of verse somewhat ignored by today's critics, but perhaps worth being reminded of:

> Thirty days hath September,
> April, June and November.

How much more easily, indeed, we've kept those thirty-day months in mind because a great unknown craftsman fashioned such musical and polished tetrameters, with their suppressed mid-beat: *Thirty days / . . . hath September*; and that jazzy caesural: *All the rest / have . . . thirty-one . . .* Certainly, rhyme and rhythm can in themselves impress on the memory even the most banal of facts or fallacies—a phenomenon all too well understood by the perpetrators of commercials.

Secondly, said Confucius, poetry can give awareness, sharpen the vision; it can help you spot that bird, as well as name it. Here we come to the phenomenon of "communication." The poet is, must be, for the moment at least, a man so intensely aware of some Thing in his universe—Frost's tuft of flowers deliberately spared by the mower—that he is driven to inventing an arrangement of words that makes others aware this Thing may exist in their universe too. That such a man chooses to communicate in *poetry* suggests that to him this medium is the most efficient for emphasis, for making people aware of something. I say, for him; someone else may want to paint or sculpt or make music from those flowers, or that ascending lark. Perhaps even the people who shoot birds and have them stuffed or eaten are really perverted poets, for whom taxidermists or cooks are only substitute publishers. And consider also that bird-killers too may have people who love them, to whom perhaps they send letters; to a special friend they might write in a sour mood (a new closed season on ducks could start it) and the sentences of their letters, before they knew what was happening, could take on mournful musical cadences, sprout sporty images, become in a fact a prose poem. You start using words to make people intensely aware of something, and you move willy-nilly into the world of poetry.

Confucius' third reason for studying or listening to poetry is perhaps as surprising as any. It's that it can "bring you nearer to being useful to your father and mother, and going on serving your sovereign." Such effects could surely have been produced only by an oriental Edgar Guest. But perhaps our philosopher is talking symbolically about the role of poetry as a preserver of traditional values, and of the heritage of the past. Certainly a great number of poets have thought that this was what they were preserving, from Vergil and the authors of the *Chanson de Roland* and of the *Beowulf* down to the late Missourian Royalist, T.S. Eliot. But what still comes over to us when we listen to the *Beowulf* is not the righteousness of homicidal Germanic tribal kings, or of early British home-life. What communicates are the powerful individual feelings of that unknown seventh-century bard, obtruding into the epic. (I don't believe, by the way, that the author of the *Beowulf* was a committee.) When he describes Grendel creeping over the moors we suddenly understand that he believed in that demon, and was afraid of the dark, and what might come gliding out of it to him any night. The poet's own primitive phobias take over, the rhythm swells, the words catch the very sounds of the nightmare—and we have a moment of great poetry.

*   *   *   *

I think there's another Confucian justification for both the writing and reading of poetry that is more valid, namely, that poetry can breed resentment against evil. An old-fashioned word, evil, but we know what he meant. One of the most quoted poems in the United States a decade ago was Kenneth Rexroth's denunciation of all its burghers for being jointly responsible for the death by alcoholism of Dylan Thomas, killed by you and me and especially by "the man in the Brooks Brother's shirt." Like Ginsberg's *Howl*, like many poems of Ferlinghetti and Corso and Karl Shapiro, these writings had much the same intention, and effect, as *Piers Plowman* had in England six hundred years ago. Indeed the vogues of Juvenal in decadent imperialist Rome, of Jean de Meun in the beginning of the long fading of French medieval Christendom, and of the Beats in the days of the collapse of western bourgeois virtues, are all the same vogue; and it was far more than a vogue. It was a means of passionate identification, by all of us, poets and non-poets, with resentment—an all-out expression of hate, hate of ourselves and detestation of the whole lousy fear-ridden world our ancestors have made, and of our own pious smug daily defence of it. Very young poets seldom express the emotion of love without mawkishness, but they are eloquent detesters, and we read them. It's one reason why Ginsberg was read by literally tens of thousands of college students, and why Bob Dylan's lyrics have been sung or listened to by millions. Their idealism is wispy, but their implicit wrath is strong.

Yet mere indignation does not make an artist of any kind, and the more obviously the poet is out to cause resentment, the more it will be roused eventually, against himself. That's the fate Kipling suffered, clever craftsman though he was. For he backed the wrong horse, resented the things the world cannot afford any longer to reject. He didn't really *like* peace, or brotherhood. "All wars are boyish, and are fought by boys," as Melville said, but it is men who make art.

*   *   *   *

The poet is always taking, and giving, a holiday from the prose of life, into a lost gone wayout beat world.

Some of this ability comes out of the general and indescribable mystery of the magical universe, as Robert Graves might put it, but not all of it, not all for any single poem, usually. Valéry, remember, said that God gives the poet one line, and the rest he must discover. And the real mystery perhaps, the real why of being a creator, is what makes a man drive on to find the other lines, in coiling frustration and self-disillusion, once the first gleam has flashed and departed. Why did Housman persist for thirteen months in looking for a final stanza to one small poem? To me it seems that the ability to persevere after the inspiration fades is the hallmark of the real artist—that everybody is or can be a poet in lines and flashes. Hart Crane was an alcoholic, but it took a dead-sober Hart Crane to hunt for hours in a dictionary to find the word "spindrift" he didn't happen to know but, finding, knew it was what he needed to perfect a single line in a poem—even though the poem had been launched earlier in a liquorous glow, and the stimulus of a Cuban rumba on a phonograph. This persistence isn't just Freud's substitute neurosis. It's the addition of hard work. I prefer Jung's view that great art rises above the narcissism of its creator.

I've been generalizing, with recklessness, about the art of others. One comes down eventually to the only surety: one's knowledge of one's own little craft. My experiences are all I have to be certain about. Let me be honest. There are times when I've sat down and merely whittled a piece of verse, to hear a shape come, then throw it away; or times when I've been piano-practising, only trying to get the hang of the form of a sestina, or the breath-accent and the heartbeat of a Black Mountain line-series. But mostly I've been impelled—impelled sometimes merely by one acute sense impression, which started a chain of recalls back to an experience which, I could now apprehend, was emotionally important for me. Or perhaps a phrase in an old diary stabbed me with a memory of October in the Kootenays, and brought me a rhythm I must always have wanted to sing, if only to myself. Most of the time these impulses have had to be suppressed in the interests of making a living. The bulk of my early poems were written in army hospitals, on buses, or in a beach shack in holiday time. But it's not always possible to suppress. The poem nags and whimpers, like one of Samuel Butler's unborn children, to be given life. In the summer of 1958 I had a glimpse of a bear and two Kashmiri men on a roadside in northern India—seen from my passing car. It was a strange sight, of course, but it haunted me for reasons far beyond oddness. The bear was huge, shaggy, Himalayan. It must have been captured high up in the cool mountains and purchased by these men with perhaps the savings of their lifetime, and they had been walking with it hundreds of miles through mountain passes down to the terrible mid-summer hot plains, brutally training it for dancing as they went, so they could make a living exhibiting it in Delhi. But it wasn't just the bear's wretchedness, it was the two men's; it was their fearful, dumb hopping around the bear. Bear and men pursued me for fourteen months till I could find the leisure on a Mediterranean Island, and the mood— and then in two hours the words came and the bearish rhythm and the images with which to lay those three ghosts, which were I think also the ghosts of my own multitudinous guilt feelings, as a well-fed western tourist in a world of unimaginable poverty and heat and dusty slaving.

Why Poetry? (II)

Marshall McLuhan, our acknowledged philosopher of communications, is also one of our unacknowledged poets. He writes in rhythms and he thinks in images. In his latest book, *Understanding Media*, McLuhan remarks that art, when it's most significant, "is a DEW line, a Distant Early Warning system that can always be relied on to tell the old culture what is beginning to happen to it." I think this is a truth not often faced, especially by Canadian literary critics, and one that must be accepted if we are to understand the creative process.

Living art, like anything else, stays alive only by changing. The young artist must constantly examine the forms and the aesthetic theories he has inherited; he must reject most of them, and he must search for new ones. Literature is all the more alive today because it is changing so rapidly. In fact it's adjusting to the possibility that the printed page is no longer the chief disseminator of ideas, and that authors must find ways to bend the new technological media to artistic purposes. The rebels and experimenters who are forcing these changes are, of course, having to fight the same battles against the same kind of academic critics who attacked the literary revolutionaries of the last generation. In their beginnings, Joyce, Kafka, Rimbaud, Rilke, Pound, Brecht, even Eliot, were pooh-poohed or ignored as cheap and sensational, as mad or frivolous destroyers of sacred tradition. Now these men are the ancient great—and the young writers who find them inadequate are getting the same treatment. Of course, many literary movements in every generation turn out to be blind alleys, but no critic should think himself so perceptive he can always tell the passing fashion from the significant breakthrough. I don't know exactly where the literary DEW line is this moment, but I'm sure it lies somewhere in the complicated world of today's little-little magazines and small-press chapbooks.

In that world you'll find that many of the poetic and prose techniques that were regarded a few years ago as merely far-out and probably inconsequential are now customary and established ones. To begin with a small example, punctuation in poetry is now used functionally only—or not at all. Syntactical ambiguities are either permitted, or obviated by artful breakings between lines, and blanks or breathing spaces between phrases. Or, if punctuation is used, it may be in company with spelling distortions and enormous variations of type faces and sizes, to signal voice tones simultaneously with visual effects, to reinforce the feeling and meaning of the poem. One Latin American poet, José Garcia Villa, is particularly known for a series of short verses he called *Comma Poems*, in which all words are separated by commas, to force the reader to accept each word as of equal importance. Here is the conclusion of one of these pieces (in which the poet has been visioning God dancing on a bed of strawberries): "Yet, He, hurt, not, the, littlest, one, / But, gave, them, ripeness, all."

Behind such apparently trivial oddities often lie serious and influential theories. Today there's been going on a great affirmation of poetry as something inescapably auditory as well as visual, a creation successful only when it conveys its maker's unique inner voice, a thing to be spoken or chanted or sung, as in the beginnings, with craft and with care, and yet still a poem in space, working on the eye. Why not give the eye as much as it can use to extend the experience of the poem? Modern photo-offset processes, for example, make it possible, without extra expense, for a poet to order almost anything visually he wants on the page, to paint his work in oriental tradition, or, following and extending on e.e. cummings, to make the poem itself a sort of etching in print, so adding both to the range and the intensity of the aesthetic communication.

From *The Creative Writer*, 1966

Index of Titles

MORE GREAT BOOKS FROM HARBOUR PUBLISHING

Rooms for Rent in the Outer Planets
Selected Poems 1962–1996
Al Purdy, edited by Sam Solecki

Three decades' worth of thought-provoking
work, including poems from the Governor
General's Award-winning *The Cariboo Horses*
to *Naked with Summer in Your Mouth.*

1-55017-148-8 · $16.95 · 6 x 9 · 152 pp

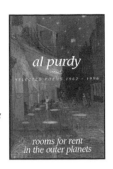

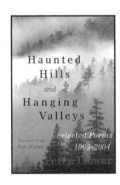

Haunted Hills and Hanging Valleys
Selected Poems 1969–2004

Peter Trower

Foreword by Don McKay

The best work of a writing career that has
drawn Trower praise as "the poet laureate of
this mountain kingdom" from Al Purdy and for
"heft and passion and a gift for telling place and
detail" from Irving Layton.

1-55017-311-1 · $18.95 · 6 x 9 · 160 pp

Selected Poems: 1977–1997
Patrick Lane

Patrick Lane, one of Canada's most acclaimed
poets, has published over twenty books of
poetry. This collection gathers together the
work of two decades, presenting his best work
as a mature poet.

1-55017-174-7 · $16.95 · 6 x 9 · 128 pp

Did I Miss Anything?
Selected Poems 1973–1993
Tom Wayman

The best of Wayman's published work from
eleven previous volumes, along with provocative
new poems, in celebration of his commitment to
honest, accessible writing with a sense of
humour.

1-55017-092-9 · $15.95 · 5.5 x 9 · 224 pp